Readability in the classroom

D1389965

For my teachers,
especially G.A.H., R.M.W. and E.A.L.

Contents

Readability in the classroom

COLIN HARRISON

University of Nottingham
School of Education

CAMBRIDGE UNIVERSITY PRESS

Cambridge
London   New York   New Rochelle
Melbourne   Sydney

Published by the Press Syndicate of the University of Cambridge
The Pitt Building, Trumpington Street, Cambridge CB2 1RP
32 East 57th Street, New York, NY 10022, USA
296 Beaconsfield Parade, Middle Park, Melbourne 3206, Australia

© Cambridge University Press 1980

First published 1980

Text set in 10/12 pt VIP Palatino,
printed and bound in Great Britain at The Pitman Press, Bath

British Library cataloguing in publication data

Harrison, Colin
Readability in the classroom.
1. Text-books – Readability
I. Title
371.32   LB3045.8   79-41794
ISBN 0 521 22712 7 hard covers
ISBN 0 521 29621 8 paperback

Preface

This book would not have been written without the support and encouragement of Eric Lunzer and Keith Gardner, co-directors of the Schools Council Effective Use of Reading project, on which I worked from 1973–76. To them, and to two other research colleagues, Terry Dolan and Mick Youngman, I am indebted for the generous help they have given in assisting me to gain some understanding of research method, statistics and computer programming.

In the specific field of readability research, I owe a great debt to George Klare and Jack Gilliland, not only for their seminal published works but also for their generous advice and assistance in tracing articles and reports. Alan Stokes of the Open University and Jeff Moule of Belper High School were also generous in giving me information on their work. I am also grateful to John Pearce for his advice and patience.

At Nottingham University we are privileged in having an outstandingly able, resourceful and cheerful staff at the Cripps Computing Centre, a number of whom have helped me with literary computing problems. Derek Bush, of Middlesex Polytechnic, generously made available his much-improved version of the STAR readability computer program, which appears as Appendix C in this book.

To all these I wish to offer a deeply-felt expression of my gratitude, and the assurance that any errors or oversights in this book should be associated with me, not them. Finally, to my wife, Rowena, I offer thanks for her tolerance, help and understanding.

How to use this book

If you want to find out how to work out a readability formula, read Chapter 3

If you want to find out when to use a formula and which one is best for your needs, read Chapter 5

If you want to find out about how to use cloze procedure, read Chapter 4

If you want to find out about producing more readable writing, read Chapter 6

If you want the issues of Chapters 3–6 put into a broader context, together with a little theory, read the Introduction, and Chapters 1 and 2

'No, Sir, do *you* read books *through*?' (Dr Johnson, 19 April 1773)

Introduction

This is a practical book. Its aim is to provide teachers, student teachers and others who have an interest in reading with a practical guide to assessing the difficulty of books in school, and matching texts to individual children or groups of children. In Chapter 5 some of the problems of measuring readability outside school are raised, but overall the emphasis is on the needs of teachers, and how they can be met.

In the report of the Bullock committee's enquiry into the teaching of English in English schools (Department of Education and Science, 1975), there are a number of references to assessing readability, but two in particular are worthy of comment here:

7.32 We therefore consider the best method of organising reading to be one where the teacher varies the experience between individual, group and class situations according to the purpose in hand. Fundamental to it all is a precise knowledge of the progress and needs of each individual child, and we consider this of such importance that it has been made the subject of a separate chapter. We can anticipate it here by saying that *a particularly important teaching skill is that of assessing the difficulty level of books by applying measures of readability*. The teacher who can do this is in a better position to match children to reading materials that answer their needs. [From Chapter 7: 'Reading in the early years'. My italics.]

15.8 . . . The effect of modern approaches in many subjects is to put a higher premium than ever on the ability to read. There is increasing use of assignment cards and worksheets. All too often these and the tasks they prescribe make no allowance for individual differences in reading ability, and *the advice given to subject departments should include a concern for readability levels in the materials being used*. [From Chapter 15: 'Organisation – the secondary school'. My italics.]

It is important to notice that the common concern in these injunctions relates to the need to take account of individual differences between children when choosing materials for them.

This is not an easy thing to do. Children have a unique personal vocabulary and store of background knowledge which will determine how they can respond to a text. Their own interests and levels of motivation will also affect how much is comprehended. Yet these factors are not always readily accessible to the teacher. General information about the child's competence in reading may be available in the form of a reading age derived from a standardised test, but as we shall see, the very concept of a reading age is under attack from certain quarters, and it is by no means a wholly reliable measure. What we need, therefore, are guidelines for deciding which aspects of the reader's competence are most important, and whether there are specific ways of taking account of them. The *reader factors* section of Chapter 1 and the greater part of Chapter 2 indicate some possible guidelines, and most of the remainder of this book suggests specific ways of implementing them.

The second quotation from the report makes it clear that the Bullock committee felt that attention to assessing readability was needed in every subject area. The report does not see the head of the English department or any other single specialist as having the task of organising reading in all subjects: at secondary level the onus is placed on individual departments to become more aware of what can be measured, and to use the information profitably. It is for this reason that a substantial chapter in this book is devoted to the special problems of assessing readability in different subject areas and for different age-groups.

The difficulty here is that of balancing the need to be specific with the need to generalise. For example, if we begin by asserting that there is a specific linguistic register within which geography texts are written, then it might be argued that we should need to have a special formula or method for estimating text difficulty in geography, because any other measure would be too crude. However, by the same token, it would not be possible to use this specific measure in another subject area, so if we wanted to compare a geography text with one from history, it could not be done. This would be a serious limitation if the intention was to select books for an integrated studies course. The overall aim in this book is to offer an account of readability measurement which is as general as possible, but with enough supporting information to alert the reader to any areas of weakness or unreliability.

The need for generalisable suggestions is in fact closely related to the revival of interest in readability measurement, in that it is when teachers move towards more heterogeneous groupings of children and more integration of subjects that the need for objective measures becomes more acute. A biology teacher might know his own subject very thoroughly and yet could find himself leading a team which was constructing an integrated science course for first-year secondary pupils. A secondary-school head of English might be well acquainted with the reading competence of bright fifth-year children, but might feel much more uncertain about choosing novels for a mixed-ability group. In both these cases teachers might wish to use an objective estimate of prose difficulty, and they would need to know that it was not subject-specific, or unreliable at certain age-levels. In a junior school the same problem might occur if a teacher wanted to analyse the difficulty of reference books in the school library. Many junior-school teachers would accept that the most difficult books in the school are those in the reference section of their library, and might wish to make an assessment of their difficulty in order that the children could be guided towards books which they could be expected to cope with, and away from ones which might be intimidating and frustrating for them. Here again the need is for an objective measure of difficulty, but one which can be applied fairly generally so that comparisons between books are valid.

The Bullock report's endorsement of increased attention to readability measurement has had a good deal of effect. Teachers have come across readability formulae as a result of within-school meetings, local authority in-service work, and university and Department of Education and Science courses. There has also been activity at national level in the UK among the various subject associations such as the Association for Science Education, and finally many student teachers are being introduced to readability formulae on their pre-service courses. All this is encouraging, in that an increased awareness of the difficulty level of many of the books and worksheets we use in school should lead to more effective and responsive teaching, but it does also give cause for some anxiety. Like all statistical tools, readability measures can be dangerous if they are misused.

Speaking to members of the United Kingdom Reading Association (UKRA), Peter Pumfrey suggested that a standardised reading test tends to go through five successive stages of acceptance and rejection. In stage one, the existence of the test is known only to a small number of specialists: researchers, psychologists and those connected with test publishing. This is followed by stage two, which is characterised by an evangelical zeal on the part of these experts, who campaign to make their colleagues aware of the advantages of the new measure, which after all would never have been designed if the tests already available did not have certain weaknesses. There follows an all-too-brief honeymoon period. In stage three, an enthusiastic and uncritical acceptance of the test leads to its being widely used, and, since it is no longer being administered by experts, the test is also misused. This leads to stage four, that of rejection. The uninitiated are accused of failing to drink deeply enough at the Pierian spring, and rather than see the abuse continued, advisers combine with those reading experts who had constructed the earlier tests (the ones which the new measure is attempting to better) to dismiss the newcomer as a dangerous upstart. Finally (and not all tests reach this) comes stage five, that of critical acceptance: the test is administered correctly to appropriate age-groups, and the results used carefully, taking into account the extent of their unreliability. Now Pumfrey's account describes how many reading tests have been received in the UK, and indeed his description would apply well beyond the reading field, but the point of repeating it here is to suggest that in the field of readability measurement, stages two, three and four are being endured simultaneously.

The quotations from the Bullock report given above are evidence of stage two (experts' evangelism), as is the number of courses on readability run for teachers by in-service training institutions.

The evidence that we are concurrently passing through stage three (that of uncritical acceptance) is abundant. Three examples will suffice. The FOG formula (Gunning 1952; for a worked example see p. 79 below) is generally regarded by researchers as a suitable measure of text difficulty with adult reading materials, but it is often used in junior schools. The results of this are inflated estimates of difficulty. For example, the FOG formula, when applied to *Johnny and Jennifer Yellow-Hat* (McCullagh, 1969), which is an introductory book in the infant series *One Two Three and Away!*, gives a US grade level of 11.3, in other words a reading level of over sixteen years. The following is an extract from the book.

> Here is Grandfather Yellow-hat.
> The Yellow-hats' house is white.
> The Yellow-hats' house
> has a yellow roof
> and a yellow door.

The reason for the FOG formula's ludicrously high reading level is a combination of two factors. First, even though the phrase structure is simple, this short book does contain two sixteen-word sentences, and these are weighted heavily in the FOG formula, thus producing a high difficulty estimate. Secondly, the FOG formula tends to produce grade-level estimates which suggest that it copes reasonably well with secondary-school and adult reading materials, but was not designed to discriminate effectively between texts at the infant and junior levels. The formula is doing its job in indicating in a general way that there may be difficulties ahead for a reader, but because of its construction it is unlikely to rate even a very simple passage as having a reading level below ten years. This does not mean it is invariably misleading, but rather that it will be of little value in the junior school unless the teacher is aware of its limitations. At present, very few teachers are aware of this bias, yet there is evidence that the FOG formula is the most widely known and used formula in the UK.

The second example of injudicious use of readability formulae is the claim of some educational publishers that, as a result of giving their authors a precise remit to include a certain percentage of long words and predetermined number of words per sentence, their texts have levels of readability precisely graded in two-month stages of difficulty. This is questionable on two grounds. First, readability measures of the formula-type were meant to be applied after the event to samples of prose – it is wrong to assume that there is an *inevitable* causal relationship between such things as sentence length and actual difficulty, and to suggest that the difficulty level of prose can be controlled in such an artificial way. Secondly, even the most widely accepted formulae have a standard error of plus-or-minus ten months, so the claim that passages can be graded by a formula into reading stages of only two months must be considered extravagant. In effect, then, the 'true' difficulty level of each passage is probably somewhere within a twenty-month band about that specified point, and it is naive to act as if this margin of error were not built into every predictive formula.

The third example of readability measures being used incautiously is perhaps the most important. In some schools there is evidence of readability data being used in such a way that children are denied access to books they wish to read, and which in fact they could read successfully. For example, a teacher might believe after using a standardised reading test that a child has a reading age of 11.0 years. A readability formula has indicated that a certain book has a level of prose difficulty of 12.0 years, i.e. that the average twelve-year-old could probably cope with it. The teacher sees the child taking the book from the shelf and, supposing a one-year difference to be too much, suggests an easier one instead. Even assuming that the book would have presented the child with a number of difficulties, this action may well have been ill-advised. At what point does a discrepancy between the reading age of a reader and the difficulty level of a text become critical? How keen was the reader to read the first book? As we shall see in Chapter 2, a person's reading ability is not a static thing, but it is measurably greater when the reader is very interested in what he or she is reading. Many teachers would say, on the basis of their classroom experience, that instruction can take children into books three or four years beyond what they are reading in other areas, and experimental evidence suggests that for a highly motivated reader a discrepancy of two years might not be too great. Readability data should not be used to deny children access to what they want to read. Rather, the data can alert us as teachers to areas of possible difficulty, and can help to ensure that we do not leave children frustrated by books or worksheets which are much more difficult to read than we had imagined.

The abuses of stage three have led to stage four, a total rejection of readability measures by many teachers and a fair number of lecturers and advisers. After commenting (justly enough) on the ugliness of the word 'readability' itself, many critics denounce anyone who considers using a predictive formula as being both gullible and insensitive, an artless believer in pseudo-statistical twaddle who ignores the many other aspects of a text which can affect how it is read and understood.

The fact that stages two, three and four are concurrent was confirmed at a national UK conference early in 1978, at which in parallel sessions one group of teachers was considering the importance of readability measurement while another group was discussing the dangerous and insidious nature of the whole business. There are good reasons for this. In primary schools in the UK, and especially since the publication of the Bullock report, there has been an increased willingness on the part of many non-specialist teachers to learn more about reading, and to help every child to become a more effective reader. Thousands of teachers each year have voluntarily taken the excellent Open University courses on reading development, and have been anxious to apply their new learning at the earliest opportunity. Similarly, in secondary schools, many subject specialists in English, social studies and science have recognised a problem and sought solutions. The rapid changes in curriculum and school organisation from 1966 to 1976 brought an urgent need for new teaching approaches and resources, and it is not surprising that a tool such as readability measurement should be used before its strengths and weaknesses had become widely known or understood. But it would be unfortunate if the errors of judgment made by some enthusiasts led to the total rejection of a potentially valuable tool, when all that is needed is more information and time for a little more reflection.

It is unnecessary to polarise the argument about whether or not readability assessment is valuable and therefore to be encouraged, or dangerous and therefore to be rejected. Readability measures have generally been devised by able researchers who have tackled the question 'What makes a text difficult?' for a number of decades. A fruitful line of questioning might therefore be 'How might these measures best be used?', 'When would it be appropriate to use them?', 'What exactly do they measure?', 'What do they fail to measure?', 'How reliable are they?', and so on. In this way Pumfrey's stage five could well be reached, that of considered critical acceptance for the test or instrument, when it is used widely but also judiciously, with a high level of awareness about any areas of weakness or imprecision.

1   What is readability?

In this chapter we begin by considering the low opinion many children have of schoolbooks. We go on to refine the notion of *difficulty* in relation to the child's own abilities and motivation, and then in relation to a number of aspects of the books themselves: legibility, illustration, vocabulary, conceptual difficulty, syntax and organisation. Finally, we consider two simple rule-of-thumb methods for estimating a book's difficulty which are widely used in British schools.

Children's opinions of schoolbooks

In 'Reading after ten' (BBC Radio 4, 8 August 1979), a group of fifteen-year-old readers told a BBC interviewer what they felt about the books they had to read in school. They were not all poor readers, but what was striking was that in general their level of motivation towards reading was very low, and this was especially so when they encountered difficulties. This is what Julie said:

> I get all annoyed, you know, and that sort of puts me off, because if I start reading a book and I come to a word I can't read, I think 'Oh, that book's too hard' and I just put it down. I don't bother about it. I don't think there are other words I can read in the book. If there's one word I can't read, I can't read the whole book.

To many secondary-school teachers the tone of this girl's comments will be very familiar. There is always the possibility that children will become fascinated by a book they are reading, and may learn what the teacher hopes will be learned. But the most likely personal response to a schoolbook is, unfortunately, boredom. This is what Ian said about reading on the above-mentioned programme:

9

I find it boring. I don't mind the work, just the books. I just don't like reading, that's all.

Lunzer and Gardner (1979) asked twelve- and fifteen-year-olds (200 in all) to judge passages from various subject areas from books in use in a different school district from their own. On a four-point scale (very interesting – fairly interesting – fairly boring – very boring) the twelve-year-olds rated six out of twenty-four passages as being very or fairly interesting while the fifteen-year-olds gave the same rating to only one out of sixteen passages.

Would these results be confirmed by a larger scale inquiry? Would the difference in proportions of passages rated as boring in the two age-groups be repeated? Why was this found? Is it because children in middle adolescence are naturally anti-establishment and reject school books as part of their rejection of school, or because fourth-year books are indeed more boring than first-year books? Is it that fourth-year books are more difficult, and they are therefore seen as being more boring? What makes a book difficult in the first place? At present, the answers to some of these questions would be guesswork, but to others our intuitions as teachers can be refined and tested by being set against the findings of researchers.

The central focus of this book is on texts rather than readers, but although a great deal of work has been done on texts, it is the reader who is our ultimate concern. Unlike some areas of psychological research (for example into semantic memory) work on readability is not 'pure' research: it is applied or it is nothing.

Why predict readability?

In the previous section, Julie said that she got annoyed when she came across a word she could not cope with. Most readers have a higher tolerance of uncertainty than Julie, but we all tend to lose heart if what we are reading seems to be too difficult or unfamiliar. The problem for us as teachers is how to predict where children are likely to find difficulties in a book or a passage. Strangely enough, even though choosing books for children is an important part of our professional competence, as individuals we tend to be rather erratic in making judgments about the difficulty level of books. It has been shown in a number of research studies (e.g. Klare, 1975a; Harrison, 1977a) that while pooled teachers' judgments are reliable and consistent, individual teachers will vary by up to six or seven years in their estimates of the age at which an average reader can read a particular passage with understanding.

Another difficulty is that of the shortage of time for finding out in the classroom which book would best suit a specific child or group. Certainly one way of finding out is to use the book with a whole group for a term, but if the book in question turns out to be far too difficult, a good deal of time may well have been wasted. Even undertaking this kind of exercise will not allow a teacher to make comparisons between books. Splitting the class into two equal groups and running what amounts to a small research enquiry will only yield information about one book, and will give no basis for deciding whether a different book might have better suited the needs of the class. Classroom trials of books take time, but they also have another potential draw-back – they are very expensive. No head of department can afford to buy a set of textbooks which will remain on the stockroom shelves because it is too difficult for the intended readers to cope with.

When planning a course of study, a teacher may not have any pupils readily available on whom to try out possible materials. Often the decisions about which books to use or to purchase need to be made during vacation times, and in any event the teacher may only have available single copies from a library or on inspection from a publisher.

For all these reasons we need some procedure which would allow us to predict in a reliable way how a particular set of readers would be likely to cope with a certain book. What we need is not something which replaces the teacher's own professional judgment, but something which extends it and makes it more reliable. We should not be affronted at being informed that, technically, teachers as individuals are rather unreliable assessors of text difficulty, because this is not really surprising. The professional experience of individual teachers varies so enormously. Every child is unique, and every group of children behaves differently from every other group. One year a class enjoys and works hard on a certain book, and the following year a similar group is inexplicably and implacably united against it.

In the UK teachers generally enjoy the freedom to choose which books to use in their own classes, and this privilege, while it enhances the range of books a child is likely to meet, also means there is less commonality in individual teachers' experience, and this perhaps contributes to judgments being made on different bases by different teachers. What is surprising is how closely pooled teachers' judgments seem to coincide, but of course it is normally even more difficult to obtain the thoughts of twenty colleagues than it is to find the opportunity to engage in classroom trials of materials.

If we do accept the need for a predictive measure or series of measures, we can turn for guidance to some of the many researchers who have examined aspects of the question 'What makes a book difficult for a certain child?'

What aspects of text difficulty can be measured?

The issue of what can be measured is perhaps less direct than that of what makes a text difficult, but it is where we need to begin. There are many imponderables in reading, and for this reason, it is important first to define the areas in which we can feel relatively sure of our ground, and then to learn as much from these as we can.

In asking 'What makes a book difficult *for a certain child?*' we are reminding ourselves that the reader's response to a book is determined by two groups of factors; one group related to his own knowledge and abilities, and another group related to the text itself.

Reader factors

The first factor which one would expect to determine how well a reader can cope with a passage is his or her overall reading ability. Unfortunately, this is by no means an easy thing to measure. Reading ability often seems to be an elusive concept, and it is sometimes more proper to define reading attainment in terms of what a particular test measures than as a 'reading age' or 'reading quotient'. As we shall see in Chapter 2, a child's reading ability sometimes appears to vary according to the nature of the test he takes. Thus, it is reasonable to talk about a nine-year-old having a reading age of nine, and to mean that one would expect him to perform on a test at a level similar to that of the average nine-year-old. What is not reasonable, and indeed misleading, is to use the phrase 'reading age of nine' to describe the attainment of every reader who obtains that same score on a test. A six-year-old and a thirteen-year-old may obtain the same number of correct answers, but they will be very different readers in terms of specific areas of weakness and in their overall language knowledge.

In considering the reader, then, we should not assume that a 'reading age' will necessarily be a reliable guide. In terms of what readability formulae measure, it is safer to interpret a predicted reading level of nine years as implying 'should be acceptable for the average nine-year-old' rather than 'should be acceptable for every reader who has a measured reading age of nine'. Two factors which would be very different in six- and thirteen-year-olds would be the level of their familiarity with written and oral language structures and the breadth of their vocabulary, and these would both be likely to produce differences in reading performance. What one might call their world knowledge would also affect how they would perform on a reading comprehension task, and it would also probably affect their level of motivation.

Many teachers have had the experience of seeing a child who had hitherto been a very poorly motivated reader suddenly become interested in a subject and then read a difficult book on it. Junior-school teachers regularly see the 'pterodactyl phenomenon' as seven- and eight-year-olds successfully struggle with a reference book on prehistoric animals. At secondary level, pupils, like Billy Casper in *A Kestrel for a Knave*, may become interested in a subject in the fourth or fifth year and read a book from choice for the first time for two or three years. They might be very weak readers, but the desire to master the book's content, be it a sociological analysis of gang warfare or a treatise on wrought ironwork, carries them through all difficulties.

Unfortunately, while a very high level of motivation can override other factors, it is too rare to render an analysis of text difficulty factors irrelevant. Klare fully accepts that motivation is an important variable in readability research, but he stresses that our response should be to consider most carefully the difficulty of texts which are read under conditions of low motivation (Klare, 1976).

Text factors

There are any number of ways of grouping the dozens of possible variables which have been used in studies of readability and comprehension, but for convenience we shall use six fairly broad headings:

> legibility of print
> illustration and colour
> vocabulary
> conceptual difficulty
> syntax
> organisation

Legibility. Some people use the term *legibility* interchangeably with *readability*, but it is less confusing to use *readability* to refer to the constellation of text factors which together determine whether a reader will be likely to find a book attractive, interesting and comprehensible. The term *legibility* is used in this book to refer to the aspects of typography which determine how readily the letters and words of the text will be deciphered. These will include such features as size of type and the particular type font used (i.e. the actual design of letters), but also lay-out variables such as line length, size of margins, leading (the space between lines), and so on. In fact, as an excellent review of the research on legibility has noted (Watts and Nisbet, 1974), the greatest problem bedevilling research in this important area is that there is a multitude of possible variables to manipulate, well over 2,000 at the last count. The result of this is that it is very difficult to compare results and draw conclusions. A researcher might do a study comparing one print size with another, while a second researcher does the same experiment and obtains different results. This could be for a number of reasons: he almost certainly varied some factors on which the first experimenter gave no information, such as leading, margin size, size of page, length of line, boldness of print, thickness of paper, colour of ink, lighting conditions and so on, any of which might have led to different results. Another major problem in legibility research is what criterion you use to assess performance. A researcher might ask his subjects to match letters which are given under reduced lighting conditions with others which are clearly visible, and compare the two type fonts in that way. But how would those results differ from those obtained in another experiment in which the subjects were asked to read the text from ever-increasing distances? A commonly used variable in this kind of work is speed of reading, but there are circumstances in which a reader might read the more legible print more slowly; for example, if he became interested in the passage and wished to savour its qualities.

Nevertheless, despite the difficulties in legibility research, there do appear to be a certain number of conclusions which can be drawn which will help us to make decisions about which books to use in school. These are as follows:

The size of type is measured in terms of point size; a point is 1/72 of an inch. This is set in *18 point*, i.e. the distance from the top of a *k* to the bottom of a *q* is 18/72 of an inch.

This is an example of *14 point.* Experimental results (see, for example, Watts and Nisbet, 1974, or Tinker, 1963), suggest that for beginning readers a point size in the range 14 point to 18 point is most effective.

This is an example of *12 point.* Type sizes in the range 12 point to 14 point are recommended for seven- to eight-year-old children.

This is an example of *11 point.* This is recommended as being the optimal size of type for ease and speed of reading with adult readers.

This is an example of *10 point.* The range 10 point to 12 point is recommended for children aged from nine to thirteen years.

Finally, this is an example of *8 point.* This is reckoned to be the smallest size of type which should be used for continuous prose, even for adult readers.

THIS IS AN EXAMPLE OF *UPPER CASE* TYPE (I.E. USING CAPITAL LETTERS ONLY). UPPER CASE IS READ MORE SLOWLY BY ADULTS AND MOST PEOPLE DISLIKE READING IT. FLUENT READERS USE OVERALL WORD SHAPE AS A CUE, AND THUS A LINE OF UPPER CASE PRINT CONTAINS FOR THEM LESS INFORMATION THAN ONE WHICH HAS THE ASCENDERS AND DESCENDERS OF LOWER CASE TYPE.

Interestingly enough, poor or beginning readers do not necessarily suffer as a result of this loss of information; in fact the reverse is the case. Upper case letters are better known by poor or beginning readers than are lower case letters, and when read singly they are more legible than lower case. For fluent readers, then, lower case is best, but for poor readers, particularly if it is wished to focus attention on individual letters, upper case may be of value.

This is an example of *sans serif* type. You will notice that it does not have the tiny strokes at the end of such letters as *r, f, l, d, t* and *q*. These strokes are known as *serifs*. A sans serif type appears to have great clarity, but in fact clarity and legibility are not necessarily synonymous, and the experimental evidence does not conclusively support sans serif type. At beginning reader level, many teachers prefer sans serif typefaces because they approximate more closely to the characters which infants will be required to write. Familiarity is also an important factor. Readers have found the typeface which they were the more familiar with to be the more legible, regardless of whether it was a serif or sans serif face. The evidence therefore appears to argue for consistency on the teacher's part, at least with beginning readers, rather than for the superiority of one form over another.

Although a great deal of experimental work has been done on lay-out factors such as leading, line width, space between words, etc., we shall not dwell on these findings because many are inconclusive, while others relate mainly to adult reading or journalism. One point which is worth making concerns the use of *unjustified* typesetting. This paragraph is printed in unjustified form, i.e. the printer has not varied the space between words to produce a straight margin down the right-hand side of the page. This may look less pleasing to the eye, but some researchers believe that an unjustified setting does help poorer readers. Many infant teachers also feel that an unjustified text with lines which end at a phrase boundary helps beginning readers, and this may equally apply to older children who are not reading fluently. This again appears to be a matter which for the teacher of fluent readers is either unimportant or essentially an aesthetic issue, but it is worth remembering if one is choosing books for infants or very poor readers.

The final point that one should make in this section is that it would be unrealistic to expect any great gains in reading speed or comprehension as a result of using more legible texts. Less legible texts do lower the reader's motivation, but more legible texts will not turn a poor reader into a good one overnight.

Illustration and colour. As any teacher knows, children like books which contain illustrations, and generally speaking, the poorer the reader the greater the value of illustrations as a motivating factor. However, as soon as we pose the question 'How useful are illustrations as an aid to learning?' we are in difficulties. In a biology textbook the illustrations and diagrams are usually an integral part of what is to be learned by the student, but in some other subjects it could be that in terms of learning, an illustration could actually be counter-productive. Watts and Nisbet (1974, pp. 82–4) quote research studies in which the illustrations were reckoned to distract the reader, who then recalled less of the verbal content of the book. This could be because verbal information is highly organised and carefully selected, while a picture, especially a photograph, contains a great deal of information, not all of which will be directly relevant to the learning task. The child needs to process this information and to select what he feels will be important for recall, and as opposed to a verbal learning task he does not necessarily have the most crucial information drawn out for him by the author of the book. In another study it was found that young children were confused by line drawings of simple objects, and in some cases they needed to be able to understand the text in order to be sure what an ambiguous drawing signified.

The use of coloured inks or paper is also difficult to evaluate in that, while it might increase motivation, it could lower legibility. Most readers would find a change from black and white pleasing, at least for a while, but technically, any colour of ink other than black, and any shade of paper other than white will lower the legibility of the print. In a decade which has seen children announce to their teacher that they want to watch colour television only, because black and white gives them a headache, it seems prudent to use colour when we can afford it, provided that the ink is a strong colour and the paper either white or a pastel shade. The news that black ink on purple paper is the least legible combination is hardly likely to cause a nervous breakdown in any school resources centre, but it might be useful to know that Tinker (1963, p. 163) found black, blue and green inks to be more legible than red or orange. The remoteness of legibility research from the classroom may be judged from the fact that no published research has been widely reported on that colour which has played a dominant role in education over the past decade – spirit duplicator purple.

Vocabulary. Ever since the nineteenth century, when the first attempts were made to describe the comparative difficulty levels of books, vocabulary has been considered to be the most important factor determining text difficulty. Surveys of readers' opinions going back to the 1930s (for a review, see Chall, 1958) support the view that vocabulary plays a large part in whether a person finds a book readable or not, and as we see in Chapter 3, research studies consistently find vocabulary to be the surest single predictor of text difficulty. There are many ways of describing or attempting to measure vocabulary difficulty, but two of the most common are word length and word frequency. Word length is usually measured in letters per word or syllables per word, and word frequency by how often the word tends to occur in ordinary usage. The longer a word is, the more likely it is to be a comparatively rare one, and vice versa. Thus, when a child complains that a book has 'too many long words', he is not simply expressing frustration at having to enunciate extra syllables; he is almost certainly making a statement about his lack of familiarity with the words used, and their meanings. Long words also tend to be abstract in their meaning, rather than concrete, and you could verify this by consulting Thorndike's list of words in common use (Thorndike and Lorge, 1944) which are arranged in order of frequency, or the more recent list compiled by Kučera and Francis (1967).

Thorndike describes his list as a 'teacher's word book' and it most certainly could be used by teachers to help them estimate the likely familiarity a class would have with the words in a particular book. One problem, however, is the time which this might take, which would be almost as great as to look up every word in a dictionary. A quicker procedure would be to use one of the shorter word lists, such as the Dale lists of 3,000 and 769 words which are included as Appendices A and B in this book. The advantage here is that in looking up words one is not attempting to compute the exact frequency of each word, and combine these frequencies in some way. The task is rather to establish whether a word is on the list or not, and this will give a fair idea of the overall vocabulary load of the text. In Chapter 3 we describe a way of using the percentage of words not on these familiar word lists to predict more specifically the difficulty level of texts.

In Chapter 6 we shall refer to the use of word frequency lists to restrict vocabulary at the authorship stage. It would be naive to assume that a sentence such as *If he is as I am, I am to be as he is* is suitable for an infant reading book, simply because it has no word of more than two letters. In normal writing most of the words which are used most frequently are ones which bind other words together: the structural elements of a sentence. For example, such words as *the, and, is, in, a, to, are* and *not* do not carry meanings in the same way as do most nouns and adjectives. They function more as operators which determine the network of relationships between the words which carry more meaning (see Kingston, 1977, for a fuller statement of this thesis). Consequently it would be ludicrous to base a children's reader on them, although the author of the beginning reader's book called *I am me* does get pretty close to this. At the stage of initial reading, word frequency is not a major problem, in that the average five-year-old will have a vocabulary of over 2,000 words on which the author can base his or her stories.

What might appear to be a confounding factor in this argument is the point that many of the most frequent nouns and verbs have a great many different meanings. For instance, *Webster's Revised Unabridged Dictionary* lists 24 meanings for *top*, and has 54 for *set*, not counting dozens more verb phrases in which it has further uses. All this might suggest that a word such as *set* might actually be more difficult to construe than a less frequently used word which at least had an unequivocal meaning. In fact, this is not the case, because these common words have a hierarchy of frequencies which operates such that the meanings which are most widely known are also the ones which are most likely to occur in print. The most frequently used words tend to be recognised more rapidly, and better understood and better remembered than unfamiliar words. It is not surprising that this variable has a central role in the measurement of readability.

Conceptual difficulty. The notion of conceptual difficulty is closely related to the more general vocabulary factor, but it should be treated separately. Word frequency is an indirect measure of abstraction, but this is not an invariable relationship. The phrase *a black hole in space* contains words which are in frequent use, *Vocab.* and yet the concept to which it refers can only be fully understood by specialists in astro-physics. The difficulty for the average reader is not one of articulating an uncommon word, or one which is unfamiliar to him. It is rather that he is in a position where he may be able to use the phrase correctly in a simple sentence, and yet he would claim that he does not understand it. A fourteen-year-old pupil might explain *refraction* by saying 'It's what happens when a stick is in water. The light bends it. That's refraction. But I don't really know what it means.' This is clearly different from saying that you do not know what *otic* means, which is simply a matter of definition. In this case the pupil is able to demonstrate that refraction is to do with light, different media, and bending, but the level of the description is inadequate, and it is this aspect of the level of analysis which is crucial.

Our problem in assessing conceptual difficulty is that we rarely have ready criteria for judging it reliably. Is refraction harder to understand than parallax? Even if we set up a series of tests with groups of young physics students it would be difficult to resolve the issue, since the decisions we took in assessing which answers were right and which were wrong would in turn determine the students' scores. In terms of readability measurement, while it has been accepted that, if anything, conceptual difficulty is more vital than all other factors, it has rarely been included in a predictive formula because it is so difficult to estimate reliably. Chall (1958, p. 46) reports a study in which a carefully constructed measure of 'idea density' failed to prove itself reliable, in that under classroom conditions it failed to discriminate between hard and easy passages. Most researchers have therefore tended to go for vocabulary measures of the type which can be applied in a fairly mechanical way. This is because an idea which is to be useful at classroom level must be one which can be applied quickly, simply, and in the same way by a variety of users.

Syntax. Most teachers would feel intuitively that the more complex a passage is in terms of its sentence structure, the harder it will be to comprehend. Consider this sentence from a science worksheet used in a mixed-ability first-year class in a secondary school:

Repeat, using the same quantities of thiosulphate solution, distilled water and acid, and the same procedure as above, only first at 30 °C, then at 40 °C, then at 50 °C, and finally at 60 °C.

In this sentence a one-word main clause, *Repeat*, precedes five subordinate clauses of various types which together are 31 words long. The main clause is in fact highly compressed. It means *Repeat the previous experiment*, and the instructions for that are 80 words long. The point here is that the sentence exemplifies two types of difficulty. A passage can be difficult if it is very complex in structure, because it puts too great a load on short-term memory and information processing capacity. However, it can also be difficult if it is too compressed, and the reader has too few clues to allow him to reconstruct the intended message quickly and correctly. In the present case, the child has to cope with both kinds of difficulty, complex structure and missing information, and one wonders whether the teacher might not have made life easier for his pupils if he had written the instructions in a style and format which were nearer those of a recipe book than a fifth-year textbook. This is not to suggest that science teachers should totally abandon the formal lan-

Table 1.1. *Five types of difficulty related to syntax*

Active versus passive verb
Active verbs are easier to read and to recall than passive verbs, and they are less likely to be misunderstood when a negative statement is made.

For example,	*The chairs were taken by the boys*
is harder than	*The boys took the chairs.*
Similarly,	*The pay-slips were not printed by the computer*
is harder than	*The computer did not print the pay-slips.*

Nominalisation versus Active verb
Active verbs are easier to comprehend and to recall than an abstract noun formed from the verb.

| For example, | *The reduction in the length of the string will produce an increase in the speed of the pendulum* |
| is harder than: | *If you reduce the length of the string you will increase the speed of the pendulum.* |

Modal verbs
Generally speaking, modal verbs such as *might, could, may* and *should* cause comprehension difficulties for poor readers, and make recall more difficult for fluent readers.

Clauses per sentence
Generally speaking, the more clauses there are in a sentence, the more difficult it is to understand.

Compression and substitution
Sentence length is not always correlated positively with text difficulty. Compression reduces sentence length but can make comprehension more difficult.

For example:	*The boat I bought was green*
may be less clear than:	*The boat which I bought was green.*
Or again:	*So did Byron*
may actually mean:	*Byron too had a club foot.*

guage of their discipline, but rather that they must be aware when they are likely to be presenting the average reader with serious problems. Worksheet instructions serve a very different function from the more expository prose of a textbook, and where the aim is to convey how to do a task, clarity and simplicity are vital. Various criteria for writing readable classroom materials are discussed in Chapter 6, but at this stage we shall restrict discussion to some of the findings of researchers concerning the aspects of syntactic complexity which appear to cause difficulties for a reader. Coleman (1968) and Dawkins (1975) have provided convenient summaries of the relevant research, and some of their findings are given in Table 1.1.

The five aspects of syntactic complexity noted in Table 1.1 represent areas of difficulty for the reader, but these are not necessarily related to flaws in the author's writing ability. A writer might well need to express a complex thought using a complex sentence structure; similarly he might need to make frequent use of modal auxiliary verbs, such as *might* and *could*. The point here is not that it is wrong to use these, but rather that children do tend to find sentences containing them difficult to understand. There are occasions, though, when simpler prose and fewer modal verbs can increase comprehension. In one study of oral lecturing (Rosenshine, 1969) it was found that an excessive proportion of qualifying words such as *rather, few, some* and *more or less* led to poorer comprehension. Similarly, the use of what were called 'probability words' such as *could be, might, usually, possibly* and *sometimes* led to haziness and vagueness. This in turn led to poorer comprehension. Lecturers who gave similar talks to parallel groups, but who avoided too many qualifiers and probability words, were more successful in conveying their ideas to their students. The injunction 'avoid vagueness' is too general to be helpful. In this experiment the results do give us specific indications as to how vagueness can be identified, and, when it is possible, avoided.

Although this section is about grammatical and structural difficulties, some points in Table 1.1 are as much concerned with meaning as with syntax. In our examples for avoiding the nominalisations *reduction* and *increase*, the meaning of the sentence is changed by adding the more familiar *you* form of the verb. This has the effect of making the vocabulary similar to that of speech, and it increases the human interest of the sentence. Similarly, the insertion of a modal auxiliary verb does not make a sentence structure very much more complex, but it most certainly does affect its meaning. We must accept, therefore, that while it is useful to consider semantic and syntactic variables separately, they do not always act independently within a sentence. They interact, often in ways which will be extremely difficult to assess experimentally.

Readers of this chapter who are well read in linguistics may be surprised that in discussing syntactic variables associated with difficulty we did not begin with a reference to the seminal work done by Chomsky (1957, 1965) on transformational generative grammar. The reason is that though his thinking has dominated work on processes of sentence understanding and production, it has tended to focus on the formal structures or implied structures of language, rather than on the factors which affect the reader's or listener's comprehension. It is certainly the case that following Chomsky, work has been done on the comprehensibility of nested, self-embedded and left- or right-branching constructions. For the classroom teacher, however, the difficulty is one of a lack of time to learn and then apply a complex structural analysis to the texts in use in school. The effort needed would be disproportionate, and it seems appropriate in this context to draw in a much more general way on linguistic and psycholinguistic research, and it is for this reason that the guidelines in Table 1.1 are offered.

The problem of obtaining a quick and reliable indication of the structural complexity of prose has led to two groups of researchers (Golub and Kidder, 1974; Botel and Granowsky, 1972) to design mechanical procedures to do the job. As we shall see, the high correlation between straightforward sentence length and structural complexity means that such formulae are not vital for predicting readability, but they are very useful in some studies. Professor Golub's syntactic density program is in fact in use at Nottingham University Computing Centre for research purposes.

Organisation. The degree of organisation within a text can affect its difficulty level, and again this is an area in which a great deal of research work has been done. Much of the work on the effects of manipulating logical or conceptual structure in a passage is perhaps too fine-grain to concern us here, in that comparative judgments of textual organisation cannot be made without a great deal of time and effort. For those seeking information on these aspects of organisation and their effect on comprehension and recall, John Carroll's authoritative review (Carroll, 1971) gives a number of useful leads.

More recently, a number of researchers have turned their attention to the internal structure of stories. Kintsch and his associates (1975) have considered the comprehension and recall of texts as a function of such variables as the number of concepts in a passage and the number of underlying basic propositions which the text contains. Mandler and Johnson (1977) have looked at the way readers tend to organise the stories they hear into a form which makes them able to be recalled readily. This line of research, which looks beyond the sentence at whole-text structure is complex but often exciting, and it could ultimately have enormous implications for textbook writing. One point most researchers agree on is that we currently lack an adequate grammar with which to represent the internal structure of stories and texts. When this becomes available, we shall have a powerful instrument for helping to analyse the effectiveness of schoolbooks. For our present purpose, however, we shall restrict ourselves to three more-transparent aspects of organisation: format variables (such as paragraphing or subheadings), the use of 'advance organisers' in a text to help the reader prepare to tackle a passage, and the use of questions printed as part of the book which are designed to promote better learning and understanding.

The research findings on the value of format variables are not entirely what we might have predicted. In one experiment it was found that readers understood a passage better when it was paragraphed according to the organisational content of the material as opposed to being presented as one unparagraphed text. Surprisingly though, another variation of this experiment, which used relevant subject headings within the passage to help the reader organise the information for himself, did not produce higher scores. It is interesting to speculate why this might be. One possibility is that by using subject headings the author demanded less critical thinking from his readers, who then read less closely than they did under the other two conditions. Another point to bear in mind is that the experiment tested comprehension and recall; in class on the other hand, what we might want is that a textbook should offer readers plenty of help in pinpointing information, and a judicious use of subheadings should certainly help. **Other studies have shown that the use of typographical effects such as bold type, underlining or italicising can be effective in improving comprehension.** Needless to say, it is recommended that such variations are not combined or overdone. For example, the use of capitals, underlining and coloured inks all at once, or for different purposes on the same page would certainly distract the reader. Another point to bear in mind is the level of the reader's sophistication. In some cases it would be worth telling potential readers that they should take account of these variations in a particular way. Perhaps readers might be told to read aloud the main points of italicised sections, or they might be told to use section headings as headings in their own note-making. It would be wrong to make the assumption that without such guidance all children can make the best use of the extra information that format variables can provide.

The term *advance organisers* was coined by Ausubel (1960) to describe introductory paragraphs which are used to help the reader by summarising the content and structure of the succeeding sections of a textbook. Ausubel's advance organisers served a more specific function in relation to the conceptual content of his passages, in that they presented general concepts which were subsequently developed more fully, or served the function of supplying bridging concepts to help the reader see how the new learning related to what he already knew. Often in an American textbook, advance organisers will be set apart from the rest of the text by being printed in italics, or by being surrounded by a border. Thus, although they are provided to help the reader's conceptual organisation, their use also implies a variation in format. A number of experimental studies have confirmed the value of advance organisers in enhancing learning, but other researchers have found that in certain circumstances 'organiser material' can be more effective when it is placed after the passage rather than before it. This is in harmony with the results of the subheading research reported above: if the organiser material has the effect of pre-empting and narrowing the subsequent reading of the child, and causes him to focus only on the material prepared for in the organiser, then he may read the whole passage less thoroughly, and end up with a poorer understanding of it than someone who was simply given the passage and told to read it carefully for a test.

A similar phenomenon appears to occur in the case of questions placed before (pre-questions), during (interspersed questions) and after (post-questions) the passages to which they relate. An impressively large and often confusing research literature suggests that on balance it is more effective to have interspersed questions or post-questions than pre-questions. Again, this seems to be because pre-questions may have the effect of encouraging readers to concentrate on certain aspects of the passage – those to which the questions directly relate – while they pay less attention to other aspects which may in reality be equally important.

It is perhaps worth noting that questions themselves differ in the extent to which they are likely to cause readers to reorganise their understanding of a text in a profitable way. Ernst Rothkopf (1970) used the term *mathemagenic* to describe activities on the part of the reader which will 'give rise to learning'. He felt that if a reader was required to operate on the text in some way, for example by answering a question, reciting a section aloud, or paraphrasing it, there was a much greater chance of the material being transferred from short-term memory into long-term memory. Clearly certain tasks or questions will cause a deeper level of mathemagenic activity, and consequently better learning. A factual question which can be answered by simply transforming a sentence from the passage almost verbatim is requiring a shallower level of processing than one which requires a paraphrase in the child's own words. The search for synonyms will tend to require a much deeper level of verbal processing, and this in turn will tend to produce better learning. This idea is not a new one, and it confirms our intuitions. What is important is the potentially striking difference between a reader's passive exposure to a text and the results of mathemagenic activities being applied to it. The concept of the 'active interrogation of a text' which is developed in the Bullock report (DES, 1975) appears to have strong support from this area of psychological research.

Relating research to classroom practice

We seem to have moved a long way from Julie, who gets 'all annoyed' when she encounters a difficult word, to Rothkopf's concept of mathemagenic activities, but the path has been a direct one. Within each of the six groups of factors an attempt has been made to set out points to bear in mind when considering the suitability of reading materials for a particular child or group of children. We have also touched upon the importance of what each reader is bringing to the text.

No-one could recall all these criteria on every occasion in which they were making a judgment about a book. Nevertheless, the attempt should be made, and the six headings given in the previous section can help to guide the assessment. When time is short, however, what is needed is a means of drawing upon the research in a quick and reliable way, and this is what formulae and other predictive measures of readability aim to do. Vocabulary is reckoned to be the single most important variable in determining difficulty, and this is included in just about every readability measure. In Chapters 2 and 3 we shall see how researchers have taken this variable into account, but first it is worth recalling two classroom procedures which are used in our schools every day, and which also measure the reader's familiarity with what is being read in an eminently practical way.

The 5% rule

This procedure uses the percentage of a child's oral reading errors as an indication of the extent to which he or she is understanding the book as a whole. If a child makes more than one uncorrected error in twenty words in oral reading then the teacher should assume that the child is finding the reading too difficult, and should be prepared to offer extra help or an easier book. This rule-of-thumb has proved its value in primary schools, particularly when teachers are wanting to make judgments about a new book. It can be extremely helpful in estimating the appropriate reading level for a newly published story while for greater reliability one can try out the book with groups of readers who are at different stages of fluency. If the first group which makes on average fewer than 5% oral reading errors is felt to have an adequate fluency in reading, then that, subject to subsequent revision, becomes the reading level of the book.

This method is well suited to the primary classroom because oral reading errors do tend to occur when children encounter words with which they are unfamiliar. However, it is a much less reliable indicator of the comprehension of older readers, particularly fluent readers. By the age of twelve the majority of readers are developing oral reading strategies which often allow them to articulate accurately and with appropriate intonation material which they can barely understand. This is certainly the case with adult fluent readers, and it seems likely that at about the age of eleven there is a shift in the psychological significance of oral reading competence which makes the 5% rule a much less valuable classroom aid.

The five-finger test

This is another very simple way of estimating how well a reader is coping with a book, and again it is one which is in common use in the early years of schooling. In contrast to the 5% rule, the onus is this time on the readers to make a judgment about their own understanding. What the children do is to put their finger on any word which they cannot articulate or cannot understand, and if they use five digits on a single page then they are encouraged to ask the teacher for help or an easier book. The five-finger test has great utility in top infant and lower junior classes, because the teacher is encouraging independence in reading while wishing to avoid situations in which a child becomes frustrated because of an experience of repeated failure. The rule encourages children to monitor their own response to material in a highly specific manner, and this is an extremely desirable goal. All too often the problem with secondary-school pupils is that they fail to ask themselves whether they are understanding a book or not. Another advantage of this little rule is that it indirectly takes account of such factors as print size and the number of lines per page, which can affect motivation and 'reading stamina'. For example, if the print is small there will be more words per page and a reader who is having difficulties will have more chance of encountering five problem words on each page.

However, except in the case of remedial groups, no-one has

seriously suggested that the rule is useful much beyond the age of nine or ten. Up to age ten, the vocabulary which children are likely to encounter in a printed book will probably be a subset of a larger class of words – those they know and can comprehend in everyday living. Beyond that age though, books serve a different function. They will increasingly contain words which the children will rarely or never use in conversation or their own writing; they will be introducing new learning and extending their vocabulary directly or indirectly. So while we must accept that too much new information will almost certainly be confusing, it is likely that words which are not understood or only partly understood will be encountered more frequently at secondary-school level. Almost by definition, therefore, a text-book will contain words and concepts which are only partly understood, and which the book is attempting to elucidate. The five-finger test will then be inappropriate on two counts. First, the question of what constitutes a problem word is by no means as simple as in the lower junior-school context, so children would find it difficult to determine for themselves whether they were understanding a word or not. Secondly, the number five as the determinant of whether a text contained too many difficulties per page might in certain cases be too low, because it fails to take account of the textbook's function of introducing new terms, labels and concepts. We should perhaps conclude, therefore, that the five-finger test or something similar to it might have a place in assessing the appropriateness of novels or stories, but it would not have general application across the curriculum at top junior and secondary level.

The intention of reminding readers of the 5% rule and five-finger test has not been to castigate these rules-of-thumb as unscientific and therefore worthless. Neither is worthless, but each method has its limitations. The notions of comprehension on which each method is based are imprecise and amorphous. Furthermore, as they stand, the measures are not predictive: they do not offer us a basis for making useful decisions about how a different group of readers will react to the same text. It is these two weaknesses in the rule-of-thumb methods which lead us to the contents of Chapters 2 and 3, for in Chapter 2 we shall attempt to delineate more precisely the nature of the relationship between readability and comprehension, and in Chapter 3 we shall examine how it is that formulae have been constructed which do allow us to make predictions about text difficulty, simply on the basis of a count of certain linguistic variables.

Chapter 2   The relationship between readability and comprehension

Much of this book is concerned with predicting text difficulty, i.e. predicting how much readers will be likely to comprehend when they read a book. In this chapter we examine what the term *comprehension* means, and how various types of comprehension test have been used as a basis for deriving predictive formulae. We also look at two factors which formulae do not measure, but which can affect comprehension: interest level and reading speed.

What is reading comprehension?

Readability is an attribute of texts; comprehension is an attribute of readers. There is therefore a fundamental difference between the two concepts. Having made the distinction though, a moment's reflection makes it clear that the concepts are intimately related, in that very often when we use the term *readability* we mean in effect the *comprehensibility* of a text. As we saw in Chapter 1, we may also be considering certain other variables, notably the extent to which a reader is likely to find a book interesting in content and legible in presentation. Most frequently however, by *readability* we are referring to those aspects of a text which make it easy for a reader to understand. There we might leave the matter, because it is easier to content ourselves with a superficial definition of the relationship between readability and comprehension than to face a rather thorny problem: that reading comprehension itself appears to be extremely difficult to define. If this is the case, it is hardly satisfactory to state baldly that estimating readability is a matter of predicting the extent of the reader's comprehension; we need to have some idea of what is meant by comprehension, and, if there are a variety of possible approaches to its definition, which ones are the most appropriate.

The problems begin with the fact that comprehension involves a whole series of major areas of psychology and psycholinguistics: it involves a number of mental processes including semantic memory, verbal learning, visual (and possibly aural) information processing, and logical reasoning, each of which is now a specialised field. There is even disagreement over such a fundamental issue as whether reading comprehension is essentially a unitary competence, i.e. a single ability, or whether it is made up of a number of discrete sub-skills which can be tested and enhanced separately. This is no mere theoretical issue, any more than physicists' debates about sub-atomic particles are merely theoretical: theoretical disputes may well produce tangible consequences, and in the present context pedagogical consequences would certainly follow from a decision to view reading comprehension as a global rather than a fragmented competence.

Despite this kind of problem though, we do appear to have a pragmatic working knowledge of what comprehension is. Mature language users are able to make judgments about whether or not they are comprehending, and if they are reading, a failure to comprehend will often be accompanied by a change in overt behaviour – the reader may go back and re-read, or scan the text more widely for clues. As J. B. Carroll (1972) has pointed out, this type of behaviour suggests that we monitor our own comprehension processes, and are generally aware of whether or not we have understood what we are reading.

It also seems generally agreed (at least in the West) that comprehension goes beyond mere decoding and appreciation of individual word meanings. As long ago as 1908, E. B. Huey, the pioneer of research into the psychology of reading, abandoned the notion of meaning as operating solely at the word level. Even in those early days of psychological research Huey felt that there was evidence available which showed that comprehension had to be considered in terms of sentence units. Smaller divisions could be considered, but these would not be apprehended as independent units of meaning, but rather as parts of a greater whole (Huey, 1968). Another powerful argument for seeing reading comprehension as a cumulative process which involves units of meaning bigger than single words is the experimental evidence cited by Frank Smith (1973, 1978a, b) in his books on reading. In one very neat experiment by Kolers (1973) bilingual Canadian subjects were asked to read aloud passages in which the text switched unpredictably from English into French and back again. With a passage such as

Un côté of the horizon s'éclairait, et, in the whiteness de crépuscule, he saw des lapins sautillant au edge of their burrows . . .

some subjects found it impossible to render the text exactly as it was written; instead, their spoken version carried on in the same language until the next phrase boundary. For example, a subject might read aloud, 'un côté de . . .' or 'in the whiteness of . . .', or 'on the edge of their burrows'. This suggests two things: that the reader is comprehending as he articulates, and that the meanings are at the very least based on word strings of phrase length. Smith would say that the reader comprehends *before* he articulates, and that he articulates what he is expecting the passage to be rather than what it actually is. This view has led Smith to make the interesting statement that reading is only incidentally visual. To put it another way, we could say that the brain tells the eye much more than the eye tells the brain. Smith's description appears extravagant, but it would seem to be technically correct. Visual information processes in the brain appear to use only a tiny fraction of the potential input received by the reader's eye (about one hundred-thousandth). In terms of information theory, the information capacity of the eye has been estimated as 4,300,000 bits per second (Weaver, 1977a); in a separate experiment the maximum silent reading processing rate of an adult was estimated as 44 bits per second. In other words, what is processed and finds its way into long-term memory storage is only a tiny part of what was originally scanned. This is just as well. The information in its full form would take up far too much storage space in the reader's memory in proportion to its value. It is far more efficient for the brain to make predictions on the basis of information received so far about the likely content of the message, and then to sample the input selectively, inspecting it more closely only if it encounters an ambiguous or unclear signal. It is in this sense that visual information is only incidental to the reading process. What

Smith said is but an instance of a broader truth, well-known to artists – *seeing* is only incidentally visual.

Measuring the reader's response

If we are seeking a workable definition of comprehension it seems unsatisfactory just to describe reading as a process whose nature is determined by the brain. On what basis does the brain 'instruct' the eye to scan the page for information, and determine each successive point of fixation? What determines whether the expectations which are built up about the text are correct or incorrect? How important are the reader's oral language habits compared with his reasoning ability? How important is the size of the reader's vocabulary? To obtain direct answers to any of these questions we need to find a way of looking inside the reader's head when he reads, and this cannot be done. The only course open to us is to elicit from the reader some response which will allow us to infer something about his mental processes and what he is understanding. To do this will usually involve changing his reading behaviour in some way, but it is a price we must pay. It is extremely difficult to design an experiment which surmounts this problem. For example, if a researcher questions a reader about a text he has just completed, the reader will reprocess what he remembers of the text. Furthermore, the extent and nature of this reprocessing will be determined by the nature of the test, so that the questions not only test what the reader has learned, but also enhance it.

Different tests may lead to very different types of processing or reprocessing, and will cause the reader to exhibit different aspects of his overall linguistic competence. There are dozens of experimental approaches, but a comprehensive description of the ones most widely used has been provided by Carroll (1972), and a simplified version of it is printed as Table 2.1. This table reminds us that there are a good many aspects to comprehension, and that a single test method will only be partially successful in clarifying the nature of the reader's response. Of the criteria in the table, those which have most commonly been used in readability work are A(a), D(a) and E(b): subjective ratings, cloze procedure and multiple-choice comprehension tests.

Klare (1963, pp. 139–44) has been a consistent advocate of the

Table 2.1. Testing comprehension: ways of eliciting a response from the reader which have been used in language research

A (a) Personal statement about one's degree of comprehension
   (b) Subjective account of meaning, main points, etc.
B Subjective assessment of whether or not a passage or statement is true or false; or equivalent to/different from another
C Asking the reader to follow instructions/directions
D Gap-filling
   (a) cloze procedure (see Chapter 4)
   (b) sentence completion test
E Answering questions
   (a) in writing
   (b) by ticking multiple-choice items
F Recognising words subsequent to reading
G Reproducing the passage
   (a) verbatim
   (b) in paraphrase form
   (c) in translation/symbolic form
   (d) 'eye–voice span' (oral reading continued briefly after light is switched off)

value of pooled subjective opinions of text difficulty in readability work, and research in this country (Harrison, 1979) has also demonstrated experimentally the consistency of pooled teachers' judgments and the unreliability of individual ratings. Different groups of twenty or so teachers were found to be in remarkably close agreement, while within groups individuals' estimates of reading levels had a range of six or seven years on each passage. Carver (1975–76) has suggested a readability scale based on small groups of raters whose reliability has been established by a pre-test. This idea has yet to gain wide acceptance, but it is an interesting one, and in the school context it reminds us that pooling ideas about the comprehensibility of books in staff or departmental meetings is likely to be very valuable, even if it cannot often be attempted.

Using comprehension tests

We would naturally assume that what we call a reading comprehension test is indeed measuring the reader's comprehension, but this is by no means a certainty. Very often a comprehension test score has much more to do with the reader's overall language competence than his close reading of the test passage. This fact has been dramatically demonstrated by Jaap Tuinman (1973–74), who used the neat idea of presenting the questions from a standard reading comprehension test to fluent readers, while omitting to give them the test passage on which the questions were based. The result should have been a small number of correct answers, no better than chance, but in the event his subjects got 67% as many correct answers as other fluent readers who *did* have access to the test passage. Clearly the no-passage group had information available which allowed them to get a good number of answers correct. Presumably this information would have been of two sorts: first, background knowledge which enabled readers to answer certain factual or vocabulary questions, and secondly, information about the passage which was passed on incidentally, from the other questions in the test.

If we wish to use comprehension tests to obtain data about the relative levels of overall language competence of a group of readers, the kind of approach described above may be very useful, and the fact that test items load heavily on the reader's background knowledge may not be a disadvantage. But if we are wanting to consider such comprehension test scores as a correlate of the amount of new information a reader has gained from a passage, they might appear to be less than adequate. This fact has led some researchers to seek a measure not of supposed comprehension but rather of *information gain*. As its name implies, an information gain score is related to how much new information a reader obtains from having access to a passage. You could describe information gain as the difference between what a reader knows before he reads a passage and what he knows after reading it. One way of measuring information gain is to give someone a comprehension test without the passage, and then to see how much better they answer when the passage is made available. Any gain score needs to be used carefully because there are certain statistical pitfalls to be avoided, but this technique does appear to have a value. Perhaps we should note, though, that this type of information gain score is still a close relative of normal comprehension test scores: we could consider it as a normal comprehension test with certain items omitted (i.e. those which individuals had answered correctly in the first testing when the passage was not available).

The comprehension tests which have been used most widely as a basis for deriving readability formulae are those of McCall and Crabbs, which date back to 1925. Since they were first published, this collection of over 300 graded reading passages has been used by researchers as a yardstick of text difficulty. In recent years individual lessons have been revised or replaced. Because the passages are carefully graded in order of difficulty, a researcher can consider the linguistic factors associated with a text's difficulty and combine them into a formula. The statistical technique of regression analysis is used to find the arithmetic equation which best expresses the relationship between linguistic variables, such as word frequency and sentence length, and the actual passage difficulty, as determined from its placement in the McCall–Crabbs tests. Because they contain so many passages, these tests give a range of difficulty which allows for a more reliable analysis of linguistic factors than would otherwise be the case. Jeanne Chall (1958, p. 28) called the McCall–Crabbs passages the best criteria yet devised for readability work.

Chall was perfectly aware of the potential weakness in this way of testing comprehension difficulty. The problem is: What is it that makes a comprehension test question difficult to answer? Is the cause a difficult passage, or could it simply be a difficult question? If questions are phrased in words which are less familiar than those which are used in the passage, readers will get fewer right than they would otherwise have done. Similarly, questions which demand a high degree of logical reasoning will often be answered less readily than questions of factual content. This is a real problem for test constructors, and standardising questions is not an easy matter. A researcher might decide to use simple questions, such as *Who fed the dog?* about a sentence such as *The prince fed the dog*. This requires the reader to perform a linguistic transformation on the question, and it would appear to be straightforward to standardise questions in this manner. However, such an approach is open to the criticism that it hardly tests comprehension at all, in that a reader could answer a similar question on *The gallytrots incrassated the brisgein* without having any idea what the sentence was about. All it shows is a familiarity with the language system of the test constructor. Thus this type of question might be very useful in a second-language examination, but it serves little purpose in testing the understanding of a reasonably competent language user.

This line of argument has led Richard Anderson (1972) to question the validity of comprehension test items which fail to examine the reader's understanding of word meanings, and his central point is that we can only test an understanding of meaning by asking the reader to search for synonyms of words or phrases in the passage. Thus a simple two-choice item such as *Is the sentence about gallytrots concerned with medieval Irish politics or fairy food?* would begin to differentiate between those who understood the sentence and those who did not. It is necessary to use the phrase 'begin to' because any reader has a 50% likelihood of being correct by chance, and only further questions or more alternative answers would reduce the chance element. Anderson's point is a valuable one, but it does not meet the objection that a test item may merely be measuring existing linguistic knowledge. Unless the passage introduced a hint that gallytrots were apparitions and brisgein the root of a plant, the only correct answers to the question would come by chance or from the reader's previous knowledge (which includes their potential as an etymological Sherlock Holmes).

All this might appear to lead us to the conclusion that multiple-choice comprehension tests are uncertain and unreliable as instruments, but this would be unwarranted.

Certainly, the specific linguistic competences which are tested in different items will vary a good deal, and the reason for our having discussed some of the different approaches to item construction is to emphasise that we cannot readily pinpoint a group of reading comprehension sub-skills which are tested by every comprehension test. Thus, in considering multiple-choice comprehension tests scores as a basis for ranking passages in order of difficulty, which is the first stage in constructing a readability formula, we must accept that it is not possible to generalise about the implied notion of comprehension which underpins the ranking. Different comprehension tests measure different abilities, and within tests different items represent different types of task for the reader. A multiple-choice comprehension test may emphasise linguistic transformations, or it may put a higher premium on vocabulary knowledge. It may require the reader to draw inferences, or it might require an understanding of figures of speech.

To a test constructor, though, questions about specific form and content may be less crucial than two other questions: these are 'How many children get the question right?' and 'Which children get it right?' If an item discriminates effectively, then not only do a reasonable proportion of children get it right, but the ones who get it right should be those who are indeed the better readers. Clearly, it is no use having an item which is so difficult that only one child in a hundred answers it correctly. Similarly, there is little point in having an item which half the respondents answer correctly if it is not the case that in general it is the good readers who have done so. For example the 'gallytrots' question would probably be answered correctly by half the respondents simply by chance. These two aspects of test items, the effectiveness with which they discriminate between good and poor readers, and their facility level (how many get the answer right) allow test constructors to gather data which by-passes to some extent the problem of exactly what aspects of comprehension are being tested. They can ask instead at what age the average child can answer a particular question correctly, and this provides a basis for making comparative judgments about the performance of children on such tests. Another way of interpreting a comprehension test score is to look at the percentage of correct answers a testee has obtained as a kind of readability index. Clearly it raises the problems of item difficulty versus text difficulty, but one can suspend judgment for a moment and work on the assumption that given a large number of items this would be a less crucial distinction. In that case, the percentage-correct score could give us a rough indication of how much of a test passage the reader has understood.

The notion of the percentage of correct answers has proved to be a useful reference point in American work on reading in a general sense, but it has also been used specifically in the prediction of readability. As a rule-of-thumb American teachers have traditionally assumed that material on which a child can correctly answer 75% of comprehension test questions is suitable for his supervised instruction. Passages on this or easier levels are said to be at the student's *instructional* level. Passages on which the reader can correctly answer 90% of test questions are said to be at the *independent* level, that is they are deemed to be suitable for study without the teacher's direct support. This distinction between the different conditions under which a book might be read is a very useful one: a survey has shown that in one large English school district there was a slight negative correlation between text difficulty and teacher support (Harrison, 1979). In other words, the harder a book was, the more likely it was that children were being required to read it independently, usually for homework. The reason was that the most difficult books were found to be those in scientific and social science courses, and these courses involved a good deal of homework reading.

The problem with the 75% and 90% criteria is that they can only be used after a test has been constructed and administered. Even if the teacher manages to construct a test which does not have variations in question difficulty, he will still need to spend a good deal of time on administering the test and marking the answers. For this reason it would be rare for teachers to set up their own comprehension exercise and calculate percentage score as a way of measuring readability. However, the criterion of a specific percentage of correct answers has been widely used by researchers in readability work, normally in conjunction with the McCall–Crabbs passages.

George Klare (1963, pp. 78–80) lists seven readability formulae which were derived from an analysis of the McCall–Crabbs passages, and in each case the criterion used was that of 50% correct answers. A formula is limited if it can do no more than to rank passages in order of difficulty; ideally, what we want is one which will assign a grade level or an age level to a passage, and this is where the 50% criterion is used. The researcher establishes the average reading level of children who can get half the comprehension questions correct on a particular passage, and over a large number of passages a pattern emerges of the relationship between the variables included in a formula and the comprehension scores of a population of children of different ages. This procedure describes in a general way the genesis of most of the best-known readability formulae. The use of the

50% criterion relates to the need to make predictions about the difficulty an average reader of a particular age would be likely to have with a specific text.

There is one case of a researcher adopting a 100% criterion, and this is Harry McLaughlin, the developer of the SMOG formula (McLaughlin, 1969), but the 50% criterion has been by far the most commonly used. McLaughlin's claim that his formula predicts the reading level necessary to ensure 'complete comprehension' has struck some researchers as bizarre, since it is difficult to be certain that anyone ever achieves total comprehension of a passage. But this is an issue to take up in Chapter 3, where the relative merits of specific formulae will be considered.

In validation studies (see Klare, 1963, for a review) whose aim was to determine the extent to which readability formulae correlated with comprehension test scores, researchers have generally found a close relationship between the two. Formulae have tended to have a correlation of between 0·60 and 0·70 with test scores. The correlations have been much higher in certain circumstances, for example when the passages on which the study was based were already graded in some way, as the books in a reading scheme would normally be, but clearly the correlation in such a case is artificially high. If the author consciously controlled sentence length and vocabulary this might produce low formulae scores, but as we shall emphasise, there is not a *necessary* connection between low formulae scores and comprehensible prose.

Other validation studies which have used pooled subjective judgments as a criterion have also generally found high correlations between experts' assessments and scores on formulae derived from comprehension test data. This double support for formulae, based on comprehension test data on the one hand and judgmental criteria on the other, explains why readability formulae are valued by many teachers and researchers. There are certain occasions when formulae are unreliable in predicting the amount of difficulty a reader will have with a passage, but this fact does not mean that formulae are worthless, but rather that the user must take care in interpreting the results.

Factors which formulae do not pick up

It cannot be stressed too strongly that readability formulae are predictive measures: they do not measure text difficulty itself. What they do is to use generally established connections between certain text factors and actual difficulty as a means of predicting difficulty in other passages. Most predictive formulae use measures of word frequency and sentence length to predict difficulty, but no formula constructor would claim a perfect correlation between what his formula measures and actual difficulty. A correlation does not imply a causal relationship (there was a high correlation between the rise in apple imports into the USA and the rise in the divorce rate, but even fundamentalists did not see this as a causal relationship), and most formulae can be 'fooled' by exceptional texts. For example, a random string of one-syllable words taken from the dictionary, with full stops placed every six words, will obtain a low reading level on a readability formula, but this will not guarantee that it is comprehensible. But neither will this example invalidate the use of the formula in normal circumstances; it is simply an invalid use of the formula.

To this extent Wilson Taylor's findings are not surprising (Taylor, 1953). He reported that readability formulae appeared to be insensitive to the actual difficulty in prose samples from James Joyce and Gertrude Stein. In his study, handpicked passages from *Finnegan's Wake* ('But who comes yond with piro on poletop?') and Gertrude Stein ('So the main is seen and the green is green . . .') successfully fooled the Flesch formula and did not correlate at all with Taylor's criterion of cloze comprehension scores. However, Taylor admits that the Stein passage is 'comparatively unintelligible', and many readers would make a similar claim about *Finnegan's Wake*. What might surprise us is not that the Flesch formula failed to rate such passages as difficult, but that Taylor used them at all to demonstrate the weaknesses of a formula approach to assessing readability. Readability formulae were derived from an analysis of the linguistic features of normal expository or narrative prose, and one must doubt the validity of applying a formula to the works of two writers who were among the greatest revolutionaries of the twentieth century in terms of their determination to remould the English language in their search for new and more powerful forms of expression. Certainly the difficulties of the Stein and Joyce passages were not accurately predicted by readability formulae, but there are two good reasons for not applying a formula to them. First, the linguistic forms of poetic writing are often generically different from those of expository prose. Secondly, we have an even less precise conception of what the term *comprehension* would mean when applied to poetic material.

In the present case, it is very interesting to note that, in Taylor's results, if the Stein and Joyce passages are dropped from the analysis, the Flesch formula scores have a correlation of 0.64 with the cloze comprehension criterion, which is consistent with most other validation studies. In his paper Taylor makes the point that his aim is not to disparage formulae, but to demonstrate that cloze procedure can measure aspects of text difficulty which are inaccessible to a mechanical formula. He also makes the point that there seems to be no positive way to identify in advance which materials are 'standard' enough to be handled reliably by a formula. What one would suggest is that in these difficult cases the issue is one of validity rather than reliability. In other words we must ask ourselves whether the sample is in expository or narrative prose, or whether it is essentially poetic, i.e. it uses language in a significantly different way from normal prose. If it is essentially poetic in form, then the application of a formula is likely to be invalid. This may or may not seem a helpful distinction to make, but it is an attempt to offer a little clarification in a difficult area to which we shall return in Chapter 5, when we come to consider the use of formulae in specific subject areas, including English. There are in fact a number of cases in which the validity of formulae needs to be carefully considered. Poetic material constitutes one, but notes, blackboard work, printed forms and examination rubrics are others which need to be considered equally carefully.

As we have already noted in Chapter 1, text factors are not the only variables which can affect the reader's comprehension. Aspects of the reader's own behaviour can be equally important, and in the next two sections we shall look briefly at two of the most important – interest level and reading speed.

The effect of interest level on comprehension

The scene is a second-year class in an urban secondary school. 'You can't make me read, Sir!' Robert used to say. 'You can make me look at a book but you can't make me read.' Sir would then attack the Lower School stockroom door (this was no doubt some kind of displacement activity) and return with another Puffin. 'Scrap dis, Sir!' Robert would say, and the first word sounded uncomfortably nearer to an abbreviated statement than a command. It was only after six months that Sir found that Robert was not a non-reader, nor even a reluctant reader. Robert was avidly reading *My Fifty Best Games* by Bobby Fischer under his desk during his hated class-reading lesson every week. If Robert was a reluctant reader, it was only to the extent that he was unwilling to read what his teacher wanted him to read.

Kevin was fifteen, two years older than Robert. He was a talkative member of a notorious group of slower learners, and he did not appear able to read any passage longer than a newspaper article. One month from the end of the school-year Kevin's teacher happened to bring into the class a social psychology paperback about a 'skinhead' gang. Kevin asked if he could borrow the 150-page book and he read it overnight. He was also able to discuss its conclusions intelligently with the teacher and to tell the rest of the class all about it a week later.

Most teachers have had similar experiences to those of Robert's and Kevin's teacher; they have seen a high degree of motivation have a marked effect on the apparent reading competence of a poor reader, and a child not only tackling a difficult text, but enjoying it and learning from it. But can it be that our ability to comprehend can be so variable, so indeterminate? One large-scale study suggests that this is most definitely the case, particularly with poorer readers.

Sidney Shnayer's important study (Shnayer, 1969) considered the comprehension abilities of 580 children aged between eleven and thirteen. After giving the children a standard comprehension test, on the basis of which he split them into seven notional ability groups, he gave each group a number of stories to read. There were comprehension questions on each story, and for each one they also had to say how interesting it was, using a four-point scale. The results were striking. Even though the initial test showed a wide and statistically significant difference in the reading abilities of each group of children, differences seemed to vanish on passages which individual children rated as very interesting. Put another way, what Shnayer found was that for all but the seventh group (which contained some children who still had fundamental problems in decoding), when children rated a passage as very interesting, their comprehension test scores were not significantly different from those of children in other groups: children who had previously been rated as poor readers performed just as well as those who were in the top group. All the children scored more highly on passages which they rated as very interesting, but there was a difference between ability groups in the effect of high interest. Shnayer found that increased motivation had a more marked effect on poorer readers than on average or fluent readers. This may have been partly due to a ceiling effect on his tests (a child who is already obtaining 80% correct answers cannot do better than to add 20% to his score, whereas a poor reader can double his score). For readability researchers and classroom teachers the implication is that the readability level is much more critical when motivation is low. It also suggests that to look for material which the children would prefer to read is not simply pandering to their whims: it is helping to get them to a stage at which they can read at their optimal level of competence, and this is something which they rarely tend to do.

How much difference does high motivation make? Shnayer's results support the widely-held theoretical view that two years is approximately the jump in reading level which a highly motivated reader can make. A difference of more than two years between the reading level of the text and the reader's normal level of competence might be too great for even a high level of motivation to overcome the problem. No doubt there are occasionally times when a child can overcome a greater discrepancy than two years, but what one is suggesting is that the teacher should be alert to the possibility of the reader's becoming bogged down or frustrated in such a case, rather than deny a keen child access to any book.

There are a number of unanswered questions about motivation: What do highly motivated readers do which is different from what they do when motivation and interest are low? Can we encourage them to do whatever it is they do more often? How could we demonstrate the answer experimentally? How important are content and style in determining motivation?

We do know something about the content factor from research as well as intuition. The Schools Council Effective Use of Reading team (Lunzer and Gardner, 1979) found in their readability survey that there were differences in interest level not only in certain subjects, but between boys and girls, and between the two age-groups used – first- and fourth-year secondary. Two hundred secondary-school pupils acted as raters, and they based their judgments on texts which had been in use with their own age-group in another school district. Within each subject there was sometimes a good deal of variation, but the following points emerged:

- At both year levels, mathematics texts were rated as the most boring reading matter.
- In all subjects, instructions for tasks, exercises, worksheets and workcards were judged to be much less interesting than factual content or narrative writing.
- Fourth-year children rated all but one of their sixteen passages (on average) as 'fairly boring'. First-year children rated six of their twenty-four passages as 'fairly interesting'. Only three fourth-year passages came up to the median interest level of the first-year passages.
- There were a number of statistically significant differences between boys' and girls' ratings. At both year levels, boys gave much lower scores than girls on passages from English lessons. Again, at both age levels, girls consistently had a lower estimate of the interest level of passages from geography than boys; this was particularly marked at fourth-year level.

Perhaps one should point out that at no stage were the children informed what subject area a passage came from; they were unprefaced and randomly ordered, and the ratings were supervised by experienced testers to ensure that there was no collaboration. These results do suggest that mathematics, English and geography teachers need to be aware of the difficulties poorly motivated readers may be working under, and in case any science colleagues are feeling their subject has come out well it should be added that the passage which was rated as the most boring of the whole forty was a worksheet from a fourth-year science lesson.

Comprehension and reading speed

A Cambridge mathematics lecturer once said that given a fortnight to work alone on his tripos papers, any undergraduate could obtain a first-class honours degree; what differentiated a brilliant student from a reasonably able student was speed – the brilliant mathematician could achieve in three hours under examination conditions what would take a lesser man two weeks to do. This is not a simple matter of accelerated cognitive functioning at the biochemical level: the increased speed is related to time needed to reconstruct a problem so that it can be handled, the breadth of previous knowledge of similar problems, and the ingenuity of the examinee in finding a suitable framework which will act as a bridge between his previous knowledge and the reconstructed problem. The time taken to solve a problem measures in a crude and indirect way the factual knowledge, conceptual frameworks and mental elasticity of the mathematician, and the reason for this digression is to suggest that the time taken to perform a reading test can be equally informative.

George Klare (1976) described the results of a review of research papers on attempts to improve readability. One might have expected that experimenters who rewrote passages to lower readability levels would find that readers who read the 'improved' version would score more highly on a comprehension test than those who were working from the 'old' passage, but this is not so. Nineteen out of the thirty-six studies reviewed by Klare had statistically significant results, but seventeen were mixed, indeterminate or not statistically significant. Why was this? Two possibilities are insensitive tests and unskilled rewriting, but another factor is reading time. Quite often reading comprehension tests are not timed, and this might mask a difference in difficulty between passages. A reader might, given unlimited time, be able to struggle towards a correct interpretation of a difficult passage, but would actually take much longer than a reader who had been given a more simply written and better organised version of the same passage. There is also another complicating factor here, which is the motivation of the person being tested. Under test conditions, a reader might struggle to grasp the meaning of impenetrable prose, when in real life he would give up in frustration. The artificially high motivation of the test situation thus might mask a real difference in comprehensibility, but if the experimenter controlled the time of the reader's exposure to the passage, there would be more chance of spotting any difference between the two versions.

It is appropriate that we should end this consideration of the relationship between readability and reading comprehension with a reference to reading in real life. Much of the early work on readability was initiated as a facet of research into journalism in the United States, and much of the continuing work is closely related to functional literacy needs, and to preparation within schools and colleges for adult life. But school too is 'real life', and every day children close books in frustration because they find them too difficult, and as teachers we can easily find ourselves lowering our expectations about how much children might be able to gain from their reading. Readability formulae will not make books more readable, but they can help us to match books to readers more effectively, and they can increase the probability that children will be able to understand what we ask them to read.

Chapter 3 How to use a formula to predict difficulty

This chapter explains nine predictive readability measures: those of Powers–Sumner–Kearl, Spache, Mugford, Fry, Dale–Chall, Flesch, Gunning (FOG), McLaughlin (SMOG) and Sticht (FORCAST). Before the worked examples on these are given, we consider two important matters, validity and reliability. What does the formula score *mean* and how *accurate* is it?

What makes a formula effective?

The number of predictive readability formulae now constructed runs into hundreds. Some have been designed by psychologists and researchers, others by classroom teachers. Many have been derived using the statistical technique of multiple regression, but others have been based on rule-of-thumb measurement and intuition. Formulae have been designed for very different purposes, and for a variety of age-groups. It would be convenient if we could make a judgment about which one formula is the best, and then forget all the others. There have certainly been enough validation studies done in the United States for us to know whether such an unequivocal recommendation is likely to emerge, and it seems clear that it will not. Nevertheless, there is no point in being mesmerised by the bewildering choice available, and two broad principles can offer us hope. First, the experts are agreed about what makes for a good formula. Secondly, unless there are good reasons to the contrary, it is worth while using formulae which have already proved their value in the classroom.

From a researcher's point of view, a good formula needs to have two crucial attributes. It must be valid, and it must also be reliable. For teachers we could add a third attribute: unless it is reasonably straightforward to apply. it is not likely to be much use in the classroom.

Validity

In seeking validity, the requirement is that what a formula predicts should in reality have a strong connection with text difficulty as measured by some other criterion; this might be, for example, subjective judgment or comprehension test scores. Most commonly this 'strong connection' is measured in terms of a correlation coefficient. A high correlation between formula scores and, say, pooled ratings of a group of experienced teachers, will suggest that a formula is doing an effective job in predicting the difficulty of the passage in question. In readability research carried out for the Schools Council Effective Use of Reading project (Lunzer and Gardner, 1979), a validation study suggested that of eight formulae under consideration, that of Dale and Chall (1948) had the highest validity, in that its predictions had a correlation of 0.77 with the criterion of pooled teacher judgments. This was the more striking because the forty passages on which the scores were computed had only been used within a four-year age-band (eleven to fifteen years).

Generally speaking in readability formula work, such high correlations have been obtained in studies which were based on a very wide age-range. In a study which looks at passages drawn from every year-group from top infant to sixth form or college level, prediction errors of a year or so either way will be less likely to lower correlations than when the same formulae are used on texts drawn from a four-year age-range. In the Effective Use of Reading project, most of the formulae studied were found to have correlations of about 0.7 with the criterion of teacher judgments, and this is very much in line with previous American research. In general terms it is therefore the case that readability formulae have good predictive validity. Of the nine ways of measuring readability which we shall examine in this chapter, seven were used in the validation study already referred to. (Of the other two, the Fry graph cannot really be considered a formula, but its results correlate very highly with those of the Flesch formula, and although the Spache formula has fared well in validation studies at primary level it was not really appropriate for secondary-school texts.) As we shall see later, each of the nine methods chosen has some merit, and each is well known in at least one field or age group.

Reliability

After validity, the next major requirement of a formula is that it should be reliable, and in this case there are three crucial aspects of reliability – how consistently the formula does its job of predicting the difficulty level of a whole passage or book on the basis of a number of samples, how accurately the teacher or researcher does the calculations, and finally, how accurately it predicts the age level of the passage under analysis. The first two aspects of reliability are usually called sampling adequacy and analyst reliability respectively, and the third we shall simply call age level accuracy.

Sampling adequacy. If we work out a readability score, unless we have analysed a passage in its entirety, we are making the assumption that there is a certain stability in the author's style. We are assuming that apart from minor variations the text is of a reasonably constant difficulty, at least in terms of what a formula can measure. This is a crucial point: if authors and their texts are not generally consistent in vocabulary and syntax, then predictions are worthless and readability measurements on anything less than the entire text are a waste of time. But this is not so. Despite interesting research by Alan Stokes (1978) on history texts, one must stress that the reason readability formulae have any currency at all is that it has been established that while there are variations between 100-word samples, larger samples of text do show acceptable stability. Klare (1963, pp. 30–1) cites two nineteenth-century works in the field of stylistics which demonstrate the remarkable consistency of an author's average sentence length. This has allowed statistical evidence to resolve some cases of disputed authorship in the literary world, and it lends support to the case that readability formulae can reliably be used to make predictions.

It is extremely difficult to generalise about appropriate sample sizes in readability analysis but in most cases formula users are advised to take as an absolute minimum three samples of 100 words each. If teachers are interested in one specific section or chapter then the samples could all be drawn from that chapter; if they are interested in predicting the reading level of the whole book then it would be more satisfactory to take one sample from near the beginning of the book, one from the middle, and one from near the end. It may well be that in certain circumstances the three results will display a good deal of variation. As a rule-of-thumb, if the range of scores for three passages (i.e. the difference between the highest and the lowest scores of the three) is more than three years, then it is wise to include another two 100-word samples, making five in all.

One tendency which researchers have noticed is that in some books the early paragraphs in a book or chapter are more difficult than those further on. This could be because there is a tendency to make philosophical or generalising statements initially, and then to go on to develop an argument using factual or anecdotal evidence later. The philosophical statements are more likely to be rated as difficult and hence the early sections of a book may have a higher readability score in terms of predicted age level. For this reason some researchers have strongly recommended that teachers should always look closely at the opening paragraphs of a book, and include them in samples for readability analysis.

In passing, we might contemplate the implication of this tendency for texts to have difficult opening paragraphs. After all, one could make out a strong case that they should be avoided at all cost: if the most difficult passage has to be tackled first, readers might be put off a book because they receive an exaggerated impression of its true difficulty. It is surely the case that an author would do better to make every attempt to gain readers' attentions initially, and then gradually increase the difficulty level. This would be consistent with the points about motivation made in Chapter 2: if motivation and comprehension are positively correlated, it will be profitable to concentrate on arousing readers' interests before introducing more difficult material. This is not pandering to children's whims. We enjoy what we are good at, and we tend to avoid what we associate with failure. Authors should take due account of this widely accepted insight, and we, as teachers, should note whether or not they have done so.

The final point concerns the analysis of texts at the sentence level. Very often we may wish to analyse comparatively brief samples of running prose, such as examination questions, worksheet instructions or glossary notes. Is it possible to obtain an estimate of readability on very short passages, or even on individual sentences? Unfortunately, the short answer is 'no'. Readability formulae were designed to be applied to whole passages of prose. If a text or worksheet has no more than 100 words, then we may reasonably analyse the whole passage, but certainly any further movement towards considering readability at the sentence level is likely to be both unreliable and invalid. It would be nonsense to go through a whole paragraph such as the present one, and say that according to the Flesch formula the first sentence could be comprehended by the average fifteen-year-old, but the next could only be comprehended by the average college student. Readability formulae do not work this way. The best we can do is to look at the overall difficulty level indicated by an analysis of the whole passage, and from this we may attempt to generalise about the book as a whole. As was stressed in the introductory chapter, vocabulary and sentence length are correlates of text difficulty, not *causes* of text difficulty, and it would be wrong to assume that the relationship is so strong that it will hold good for each sentence individually. If we wish to consider text difficulty at the individual sentence level, then it is appropriate to set aside formulae, and to do one of three things: (a) to consider vocabulary difficulty alone using a word-frequency list (see, for example, the work of Elley, 1969); (b) to examine syntax using the table in Chapter 1 (see p. 23); (c) to monitor closely the comprehensibility of the materials as they are used by children in the classroom.

Analyst reliability. When teachers work out a readability score we would naturally expect that they should obtain the same result as colleagues using the same passage and formula. If this does not happen, the implication is that the teachers are producing unreliable results. A variety of reasons could account for this.

First, it could be that the formula itself includes a variable about which it is very difficult to make consistent judgments, such as the *ratio of abstract to concrete words*. This is the kind of variable which we intuitively feel is an extremely good indicator of vocabulary difficulty. The more simple concrete words there are in a passage, the easier it is to read and understand; the more abstract words, the harder it is likely to be to understand. Thus, the ratio of abstract to concrete words would appear to be a worthwhile variable for inclusion in a predictive formula. However, how reliably can we classify an abstract noun? Consider the nouns *salt, solution* and *acid*. Each of these words is in everyday use, and yet in an advanced chemistry course they could be defined at the molecular level in terms which would suggest that they were abstract concepts. In certain circumstances, therefore, whether a noun is concrete or abstract is not clear unless we consider the context in which it is used, and even then there may be a doubt which would lead one teacher to rate a word as abstract and another to assess it as concrete. Rudolf Flesch did in fact design a formula (Flesch, 1950) which included a ratio of concrete to abstract words, but it is generally considered to be rather unwieldy and is therefore not included in this book.

Other variables which might tend to produce unreliable results are imprecise ones such as *ideas per 100 words*, or variables which require judgments about grammatical classes, such as *prepositional phrases per 100 words* or *number of indeterminate clauses*. Syntax variables are likely to be scored unreliably either because experts might disagree about scoring certain sentences, or simply because the average teacher's recall of formal grammar may be untrustworthy. In this chapter, therefore, we shall not introduce any formulae which present problems of reliability in that they require many subjective decisions. The only indirect syntactic variable used here is the number of words per sentence, and provided that we work to an operational definition of a word as a string of characters delineated by spaces, and a sentence as a string of words delineated by a full stop, exclamation mark or question mark, then we should eliminate most of the potential unreliability which could be associated with this variable. The only other source of analyst unreliability would be a simple counting error.

Vocabulary variables do present slightly more of a problem. Broadly speaking, one can use two methods of estimating vocabulary complexity: a measure of the proportion of words which are on a particular word-frequency list, or a count based on the number of syllables per word in a passage. With some word-frequency lists, the potential unreliability is related to the confusion a teacher might have in interpreting the rules which determine whether or not a specific word is to be regarded as 'familiar' or not. The Dale–Chall formula has over 30 rules for deciding whether or not a specific word is to be regarded as familiar, i.e. whether it is on the list of the 3,000 words best-known by American eight-year-olds. For example, regular verb forms such as *stopped* are regarded as familiar, even though only *stop* is on the list itself. It is important therefore that users of the Dale–Chall formula familiarise themselves with these rules and apply them consistently, otherwise they might rate too many words as unfamiliar and obtain exaggerated difficulty scores for the passages they analyse.

One method of determining whether or not a variable can be scored unequivocally is to consider whether a computer can do the job. The Dale–Chall formula is rather complex, but in the United Kingdom and in the United States computer versions of the formula exist, and they test with over 99% accuracy whether or not each word in a passage is to be counted as familiar, so the formula can be viewed as reliable in those terms.

Computers cannot read aloud, but they are fairly accurate at counting syllables, in that with a few exceptions (and these can readily be taken account of) each occurrence of a vowel in a word is equivalent to one syllable. Most computer programs which estimate the number of syllables in words do in fact make a few errors per 1,000 words, but these are not all in the same direction and tend to cancel each other out. In contrast, human raters can be embarrassingly inaccurate, usually in overestimating the number of syllables in words, and can produce as a result highly unreliable scores.

Why are syllable counts included in so many readability formulae? The answer is that they are a quick method of measuring word length, and word length is itself a correlate of word frequency. A count of the average number of three-syllable words per 100 words is thus a good indicator of vocabulary difficulty, and is generally quicker to make than checking words on a word list, or counting the number of letters in every word. Counting is not a problem for a computer, of course, and there are signs that new formulae will drop the notion of counting syllables and concentrate on letter counts, which are quicker in terms of computer time and also more reliable.

Age level accuracy. A readability formula may have high validity in terms of its correlation with another criterion of difficulty such as comprehension test scores, but this is no guarantee of its accuracy in predicting age levels for appropriate classroom use. As can be seen from Table 3.1, in the Effective Use of Reading

Table 3.1. Average reading levels (in years) obtained from formulae compared with pooled teachers' assessments (differences shown in brackets)

	First-year secondary texts	Fourth-year secondary texts
Pooled teacher assessments	11.30	13.14
Dale–Chall formula	11.88 (+ 0.58)	13.04 (− 0.10)
Mugford formula and chart	11.50 (+ 0.20)	13.59 (+ 0.45)
Flesch formula	12.23 (+ 0.93)	14.21 (+ 1.07)
Powers–Sumner–Kearl formula	10.09 (− 1.21)	10.76 (− 2.38)
FORCAST formula	13.76 (+ 2.46)	14.46 (+ 1.32)
SMOG formula	13.23 (+ 1.93)	15.12 (+ 1.98)
FOG formula	13.95 (+ 2.65)	16.37 (+ 3.23)

Data from the Effective Use of Reading project (Lunzer and Gardner, 1979)
Sample sizes: 24 first-year texts; 16 fourth-year texts

project survey of texts in use in ten schools one formula gave consistently low age level ratings. The formula developed by Powers, Sumner and Kearl (1958) as a recalculation of the Flesch formula only ranged in mean scores from 10.09 years to 10.76 years for groups of texts which were taken from first-year and fourth-year secondary classes respectively. In the validation study on the same project this formula fared well, having a correlation of 0.73 with the criterion of pooled teacher judgments, but it would be almost worthless at secondary level in readability assessment because it barely differentiates between different texts.

This example of a formula which discriminates poorly at secondary level serves to remind us that no formula yet devised is equally effective at all levels from top infant to top secondary. If a formula was initially constructed on the basis of correlations with text difficulty at a certain age level, then it will be at that same age level that it is at its most effective. The Powers,

Sumner and Kearl recalculation of the Flesch formula is very useful at lower primary level, but is not accurate beyond a 'true' reading level of about ten years. Much the same can be said of the Spache formula (Spache, 1953), which was originally designed for use on material for children in US schools, in grades 1–3, which corresponds to British top infant and lower junior classes. This has been included because it too is valuable at junior level, and primary teachers will thus be offered in this chapter a choice of two formulae to work with – one which has very high validity (the Spache formula), and one which is relatively quick to compute and nevertheless also has fairly high validity (the Powers, Sumner and Kearl recalculation of the Flesch formula).

While it is true to say that no formula can claim total age level accuracy, the Fry graph (Fry, 1977) is quite effective in age level prediction, even though it does not produce a precise numerical age. The Fry graph has been used successfully at every level from infant to top secondary, and in previous studies it has been found to correlate extremely highly with the Flesch formula, which is generally considered to be the best of the formulae which do not use a word list.

From Table 3.1 it can also be seen that in the Effective Use of Reading study the two measures which had the highest age level accuracy in relation to teachers' judgments were the Dale–Chall and Mugford formulae. These were the only formulae which had an average of less than half a year's difference when compared with pooled teacher judgments; indeed the other formulae had average discrepancies of between one and three years on every passage. In fairness to McLaughlin, one should point out that his SMOG formula does claim a criterion of 'total comprehension', and therefore one would expect his scores to be somewhat high, but this explanation could not be applied to the FORCAST and FOG formulae, which do appear to be unrealistically high in certain cases.

In general terms, a reading level of, say, ten years suggests that in terms of what a formula measures a passage should be comprehensible to the average ten-year-old. We must not forget that an eight-year-old with a reading age of ten on a standardised test is not the same as a fifteen-year-old with a reading age of ten. Their needs and interests will differ, and it is in an effort to avoid any possible misuse of the concept of reading age that the term *reading level* is used in this book. Nevertheless, even with this restricted use of the term *reading level*, we encounter problems with formulae which produce scores of above sixteen years. It may be, for example, that the reading ability of the average adult is not significantly higher than that of the average sixteen-year-old. Indeed it may be that the average 21-year-old is a poorer reader than the average sixteen-year-old. To this extent a readability score of 20 or 25 years on a difficult passage is meaningless. We could adopt the convention that the age should be taken to imply 'could be read successfully *by the average adult in full-time education*'. Thus a reading level of 20 would imply second-year undergraduate work at university or college, and a score of 25 would suggest Master's degree work, not what could be read by the average 25-year-old. No formulae yet devised have been thoroughly validated on this kind of material, and it would be a difficult task for any researcher to undertake. If, therefore, high reading level scores are interpreted in relation to the age of students in full-time education, a teacher should recognise that the decision is a slightly arbitrary one, and the validity of the measurement is not fully established.

Which formula? A consumer's guide

One of the besetting problems in readability work is the difficulty of balancing relative strengths and weaknesses when coming to a decision about which formula to use. In validation research the Dale–Chall formula has been found to be the best in studies made on both sides of the Atlantic. Why, therefore, is it not the only one in use? The reason is that it is also the most tedious to work out, and many teachers have understandably preferred to use easier but slightly less valid measures. What teachers need to know is how much is being lost in terms of validity when they seek a formula which is easier to apply. Similarly, a formula may have high validity and may be easy to apply, but it could have poor age level accuracy. In an effort to assist formula users to make judgments, Table 3.2 offers in comparative form data about validity, accuracy and ease of application.

It can be a highly dangerous business to pool research results

Table 3.2. Summary of research data on nine readability measures, and ratings of ease of application

	Validity	Age level accuracy (8–16 age-range)	Ease of application
Flesch formula (Grade score)	●●●●	●●●	●●
Fry graph	●●●●	●●●	●●●
Powers–Sumner–Kearl formula	●●●●	●	●●●
Mugford formula and chart	●●●●	●●●●	●●
FOG formula	●●●	●●	●●●●
SMOG formula	●●●	●●	●●●●●
Dale–Chall formula	●●●●●	●●●●	●
Spache formula	●●●●	●●	●●
FORCAST formula	●●	●●	●●●●

Key: the more blobs the better

from different studies. Some experiments are conducted far more efficiently than others, and may have been designed using very different materials or subjects. Nevertheless, because the experimental evidence is relatively inaccessible for British teachers, and because the aim of this book is to clarify practical issues in the use of formulae, the table includes a section on validity which pools data from a number of sources. Essentially, the assessment of validity takes into account the strength of the correlations which have been found between the formula and another measure of text difficulty such as comprehension test scores. If a number of independent studies have concurred in finding good validity, this has also been taken into account. In effect the validation data has come from three sources: an initial research paper; subsequent cross-validation studies by other researchers or the author himself; the validation study carried out on the Effective Use of Reading project, which at some point used all except the Spache formula in a comparative study. The section in the table on age level accuracy draws heavily on the Effective Use of Reading project work, particularly the results on closeness to teachers' estimates which were shown in Table 3.1. One should point out that the age level accuracy rating assumes a range of difficulty going from middle junior to upper secondary level, i.e. the approximate age range eight to sixteen years.

As is made clear in later sections, the Powers, Sumner and Kearl formula and the Spache formula fare poorly because they do not discriminate well above junior level. This does not mean that they should be totally rejected. The section on ease of application drew upon the comments of teachers on in-service courses who had tried their hand at calculating various formula scores. I also timed the tallying and calculating needed to produce readability scores on a variety of passages, and these results were incorporated in the final ratings.

The less time a teacher can find for calculating readability results, the more important ease of application becomes. None of the formulae included in Table 3.2 fails to gain four blobs on at least one section, and four formulae gain a total of ten. These are the Fry graph, the Mugford method, the SMOG formula and the Dale–Chall formula. Each of the others does have a virtue, however. The Flesch formula is the most widely known, and the nomogram (Figure 3.5) offers a quicker method of obtaining an age level than is normally possible. The Powers–Sumner–Kearl and Spache formulae would obtain higher age level accuracy scores on an age range of five to ten years, and this would make them as good as any on infant and junior texts. The FOG formula is very simple to compute in that, as in the SMOG formula, the vocabulary variable requires the analyst only to count the number of words which have more than three syllables, and this is much easier than counting every syllable. Finally, the FORCAST formula does not involve any syntax variable: this means that sentence length does not need to be computed, and again makes the formula a relatively quick one to work out. This in turn suggests that the formula is well suited to materials such as adult technical manuals in which technical terms are the crucial variable and sentence structure is much less important (or indeed very difficult to identify).

How to use the formulae

In the following sections worked examples demonstrate the calculation of each of the nine formulae which have been discussed so far, and which on the basis of the available evidence would seem to be potentially the most useful in the classroom.

Two passages have been chosen as a basis for the calculations.

Table 3.3. Counts of linguistic variables on Texts A and B

Linguistic variable	Text A. Iron age clothing			Text B. The nitrogen problem		
	Sample 1	Sample 2	Sample 3	Sample 1	Sample 2	Sample 3
Words per sentence	15.9	18.2	11.5	17.2	12.5	17.2
Sentences per 100 words	6.3	5.5	8.7	5.8	8.0	5.8
Syllables per 100 words	121	113	117	169	178	156
Syllables per word	1.21	1.13	1.17	1.69	1.78	1.56
Monosyllabic words per 100 words	80	87	85	56	55	65
Monosyllabic words per 150 words[1]	$(80 + 87 + 85) \div 2 = 126$			$(56 + 55 + 65) \div 2 = 88$		
Polysyllabic words per 100 words	1	0	2	18	26	16
Polysyllabic words per 30 sentences[2]	$(30 \times 3) \div 22 = 4.09$			$(30 \times 60) \div 20 = 90.0$		
% of words not on 769 list	18	14	19	27	29	28
% not on 3,000 list	7	3	6	24	26	21
Mugford word length score	60	38	48	115	124	114

Polysyllabic words = words of three or more syllables

Note 1. Monosyllabic words per 150 words extrapolated from scores on three 100-word samples

Note 2. Polysyllabic words per 30 sentences extrapolated from scores on total passage analysed (for Text A, 3 in 22 sentences; for Text B, 60 in 20 sentences)

Table 3.4. Readability formulae results for Texts A and B

| | Text A. Iron age clothing | | | | Text. B. The nitrogen problem | | | |
	Sample 1	Sample 2	Sample 3	Mean	Sample 1	Sample 2	Sample 3	Mean
Powers–Sumner–Kearl	9.53	9.35	9.02	9.30	11.82	11.87	11.23	11.64
Spache	9.06	9.01	8.61	8.89	9.95	9.55	10.03	9.84
Mugford	10	8.5	8.5	9.0	18	17	18	17.7
Fry graph	11	11	8	10	18	*	15	17
Dale–Chall	10.53	10.01	10.31	10.28	14.07	13.99	13.12	13.73
Flesch	11.16	10.72	10.39	10.76	19.05	19.48	15.69	18.07
FOG	11.72	12.28	10.40	11.47	19.08	20.40	18.28	19.25
SMOG	*	*	*	10	*	*	*	17
FORCAST	*	*	*	12.40	*	*	*	16.20

* Scores could not be determined for these sub-samples.

Text A, 'Iron age clothing', is taken from a book which was in use with a mixed-ability class of twelve-year-olds in a secondary school, and Text B, 'The nitrogen problem', is from a pamphlet used for background reading in a fourth-year secondary-school science class. The texts are printed on pages 82 and 83.

In order to avoid unnecessary repetition, counts of such linguistic variables as number of syllables per 100 words, or words per sentence, which are used in calculating the formula scores, are presented together in Table 3.3. In each text sample, an oblique stroke follows the hundredth word, and the calculations are based on the words up to that point. Those who have not used a readability formula before may wish to repeat some of the calculations based on the sample texts in order to check their own analyst reliability.

Counting words

Not all researchers agree on what constitutes a word, but unless otherwise specified, the definition we shall adopt is a pragmatic and consistent one: *a word is a string of letters or characters delimited by spaces*, i.e. with a space at each end. Thus, hyphenated words, numbers such as *15.9, 1964—65* and abbreviations such as *M.Sc.* would all be counted as single words.

Counting syllables

Generally speaking, each vowel sounded in a word corresponds to one syllable. So in the words *Jan, met, Jim, for, but,* and *cry* each vowel (*a, e, i, o, u, y*) corresponds to a single syllable. Longer words such as *straight, write, which, splice* or *boot* still only count as one syllable, since there is only one vowel sound in each (*ay, eye, i, eye, oo*). Words ending in *-ed* may look as if they should have more than one syllable, but this is rarely the case. Think of *combed, guessed,* or *grouped*. In each there is still only one vowel sound.

Two sorts of word will present problems, and these are ambiguous cases and abbreviations. For example, is *piano* three syllables or two? Is *visual* three syllables or two? Is *iron* one syllable or two? There are no fixed answers to these questions, since pronunciation will vary according to differences in accent. The simplest expedient is to read the word aloud and listen to yourself, and to make the judgment on that basis. Given practice, and especially if you compare notes with a colleague, you will quickly become reliable.

The matter of abbreviations is slightly more difficult. Edward Fry (1977) suggests that each character is scored as one syllable, so *U.K.R.A.* would be four and *U.N.E.S.C.O.* six. Numerals can be treated in the same way, so *1980* is counted as four syllables and *285,773* as six. This is a straightforward and sensible system, but it has one flaw, which is that it presupposes that the scorer can differentiate between words and non-words, and this is a serious problem for a computer. Most computer programs count syllables by counting vowels, and then implementing a brief set of rules to deal with *-ed* endings, diphthongs and so on. If no vowels are encountered, the program allocates by default a minimum value of one syllable to a non-word or string of characters. This bypasses the problem of having to signal occurrences of non-words in some special way, and it gives an even simpler rule for dealing with abbreviations, numerals and non-word strings of characters: *count non-words as one syllable*. This is reliable in that it treats all non-words the same way, and avoids disagreements over whether we count *163* as three or seven syllables, and find that non-word strings are artificially increasing the measure of vocabulary difficult in a text.

Counting sentences

The next problem is to determine the number of words per sentence. Should this be based on complete sentences, or on the 100 words alone, and if so, how is the fraction of the last sentence to be decided? Since we are going to average out the scores on three samples it is, strictly speaking, preferable that the samples should all be of equal length, otherwise the samples will contribute unequally to the final score. We cannot therefore simply work from the end of the sentence which is running at word 100, at least not directly. The solution is to consider the part of the sentence up to word 100 as a fraction of its total length, and then to add this to the number of complete sentences. Thus in Text A, Sample 1, there are six complete sentences before the oblique stroke, followed by nine words of a 30-word sentence. The total number of sentences per hundred words is therefore $6\frac{9}{30}$, and if we divide this figure into 100 we obtain the average number of words per sentence.

Accuracy in calculation
When calculating the formulae, work to three decimal places throughout. Round the *final* result to one decimal place.

The Powers–Sumner–Kearl formula (1958)

This is a relatively simple formula to work out, and although it produces few reading levels below seven years, it is more suitable for primary schoolbooks than its better-known relative, the Flesch formula. The Powers–Sumner–Kearl formula is not suitable for secondary texts because it exhibits a marked ceiling effect, and will rarely produce a reading level above twelve, even on difficult material. The formula is:

$$\text{US grade} = -2.2029 + (0.0778 \times \text{WDS/SEN})$$
$$+ (0.0455 \times \text{SYLL/100w})$$

where WDS/SEN = average number of words per sentence and SYLL/100w = average number of syllables per 100 words
UK reading level (in years) = US grade + 5

The Spache formula (1953)

This formula has been used widely in the United Kingdom, and provided that the user is aware that the formula is unreliable with books above a true difficulty level of eleven years, there is no reason why this should not continue. The vocabulary variable, percentage of unfamiliar words (i.e. words not derived from words on Dale's 769 word list – see Appendix B), takes time to work out but it tends to produce more accurate scores than those from the Powers–Sumner–Kearl formula. The Spache formula is:

$$\text{US grade} = (0.121 \times \text{WDS/SEN})$$
$$+ (0.082 \times \text{PERCENT UFMWDS})$$
$$+ 0.659$$

where WDS/SEN = average number of words per sentence and UFMWDS = unfamiliar words
UK reading level (in years) = US grade + 5

Deciding whether or not a word is to be regarded as 'familiar' is not always easy. The following guidelines were written by Diana Bentley of the University of Reading reading centre to help teachers to work out the Spache formula. They may seem a little complex but in fact they are soon mastered.

- Count all letters and numbers in figures as familiar.
- Proper nouns, or names of persons, places, are counted as familiar.
- Count regular verb forms of words on the list as familiar. This includes only *-ing, -es, -s, -ed* and those changes involving doubling of the final consonant, or dropping the final *e* or changing *y* to *i* when adding a suffix. Derivatives of verbs involving internal changes in spelling, as *ride—rode, buy—bought, break—broke*, are not familiar unless on the list. Verbs changed to nouns by adding a suffix are not familiar unless on the list.
- Count regular plurals and possessive endings of nouns as familiar. Plurals in *-s, -es,-ies* are familiar; irregularly formed plurals, as in *ox–oxen, goose–geese*, are unfamiliar unless on the list.
- Derivatives of verbs that function as a noun or adjective, as *build–building, burn–burnt*, or nouns that are changed to function as an adjective, as *sleep–sleepy, sun–sunny, bravery–brave*, are not familiar unless on the list.
- Adjectival or adverbial endings as *-ly, -est, -er, ily* are considered familiar when the base word is on the list. For example, *big, bigger, biggest*, or *brave, bravely, braver, bravest* are all considered familiar since *big* and *brave* are on the list.
- Count a word as unfamiliar only once even though it appears again or with variable endings later in the sample.
- A group of words, consisting of the repetition of a single word or exclamation, as *oh, oh, oh* and *look, look, look*, is counted as a single sentence regardless of punctuation.
- Count hyphenated words as unfamiliar unless both parts appear in the word list.
- Count contractions, as *didn't*, unfamiliar unless on the list.
- Count hyphenated words, compound words and numbers in figures as one word.

The Mugford chart (1970)

Leonard Mugford's chart is the best of the 'intuitively' derived readability measures. It is the product of years of research and classroom trials, and its letters-per-word variable takes account of difficulties in monosyllabic words like *strength* which many formulae would ignore. This is how you work it out.

Count a 100-word sample. Treat words joined by hyphens, e.g. *boat-house*, as separate words. Count contracted forms, such as *wouldn't*, as one word only. Count each number expressed in figures as a word.

Make four lists of the words in the sample. *List 1* contains the polysyllabic words (i.e. words of three or more syllables). *List 2* consists of the non-polysyllabic words (i.e. words of one or two syllables) seven or more letters long. *Lists 3* and *4* contain respectively the six-letter and five-letter non-polysyllabic words. Do not list the same word more than once, but always count derived forms separately from their base words; e.g. *child, children, children's* would all be listed separately. Proper

Figure 3.1. The Mugford readability chart: word length section
© Leonard Mugford 1970

Number of words in list	List 1	List 2	List 3	List 4
1	4	2	2	1
2	8	5	3	2
3	12	7	5	3
4	16	10	6	4
5	20	12	8	5
6	24	15	9	6
7	28	17	11	7
8	32	20	12	8
9	36	22	14	9
10	40	25	15	10
11	44	27	17	11
12	48	30	18	12
13	52	32	20	13
14	56	35	21	14
15	60	37	23	15
16	64	40	24	16
17	68	42	26	17
18	72	45	27	18
19	76	47	29	19
20	80	50	30	20
21	84	52	32	21
22	88	55	33	22
23	92	57	35	23
24	96	60	36	24
25	100	62	38	25
26	104	65	39	26
27	108	67	41	27
28	112	70	42	28
29	116	72	44	29
30	120	75	45	30

nouns, nonsense words, representations of animal noises, etc. should be classified in the same way as ordinary words, but numbers expressed in figures should not be listed.

When you have worked through the entire sample, count the number of words in each list. Find the word length score for each list from Figure 3.1, and then add these scores together to obtain the word length score for the passage. For example, an analysis of Text B, Sample 3, yields 14 words in list 1, 6 words in list 2, 10 words in list 3 and 8 words in list 4, giving a word length score

$$56 + 15 + 15 + 8 = 114$$

Count the number of sentences. Note that

'Come here!' John shouted.
'Who is it?' he asked.

would each count as *one* sentence only.

Figure 3.2. The Mugford readability chart: conversion table
© Leonard Mugford 1970

Number of sentences					Difficulty index
7 or more	6	5	4	3 or fewer	
142–146	133–137	124–128	115–119	107–110	20
136–141	128–132	119–123	111–114	102–106	19
130–135	122–127	114–118	106–110	98–101	18
124–129	116–121	108–113	101–105	93–97	17
117–123	110–115	103–107	95–100	88– 92	16
112–116	105–109	98–102	91–94	84–87	15
108–111	101–104	95–97	88–90	81–83	14.5
104–107	98–100	91–94	85–87	78–80	14.0
101–103	94–97	88–90	82–84	75–77	13.5
96–100	90–93	84–87	78–81	72–74	13.0
92–95	86–89	81–83	75–77	69–71	12.5
88–91	82–85	77–80	71–74	66–68	12.0
83–87	78–81	73–76	68–70	62–65	11.5
80–82	75–77	70–72	65–67	60–61	11.0
79	74	69	64	59	10.9
78	73	68	63	–	10.8
77	72	67	–	58	10.7
76	71	66	62	57	10.6
75	70	–	61	56	10.5
74	69	65	60	55	10.4
73	68	64	59	–	10.3
71–72	67	63	58	54	10.2
70	66	62	57	53	10.1
69	65	61	56	52	10.0

Number of sentences					
7 or more	6	5	4	3 or fewer	Difficulty index
68	64	60	55	51	9.9
67	63	59	54	50	9.8
66	62	57–58	53	49	9.7
64–65	60–61	56	52	48	9.6
63	59	55	51	47	9.5
62	58	54	50	46	9.4
61	57	53	49	45	9.3
59–60	55–56	52	48	44	9.2
58	54	51	47	43	9.1
56–57	53	49–50	46	42	9.0
55	52	48	45	41	8.9
53–54	50–51	47	43–44	40	8.8
52	49	45–46	42	39	8.7
50–51	47–48	44	41	38	8.6
49	46	43	40	37	8.5
47–48	44–45	41–42	38–39	35–36	8.4
45–46	42–43	40	37	34	8.3
43–44	41	38–39	35–36	33	8.2
41–42	39–40	36–37	34	31–32	8.1
39–40	37–38	35	32–33	30	8.0
37–38	35–36	33–34	30–31	28–29	7.9
35–36	33–34	31–32	29	26–27	7.8
33–34	31–32	29–30	27–28	25	7.7
30–32	28–30	26–28	25–26	23–24	7.6
27–29	26–27	24–25	22–24	0–22	7.5
24–26	23–25	21–23	0–21		7.4
21–23	19–22	0–20			7.3
18–20	0–18				7.2
0–17					7.2 or less

Find the difficulty index for the sample from Figure 3.2. Look down the appropriate column until you encounter the sample's word length score. The sample's difficulty index is on the same row. Difficulty indices of less than 16 can be regarded as UK reading levels (US grade = UK reading level −5).

If the difficulty index is '7.2 or less', make a single list of all the different words in the passage. Be careful not to list the same word more than once! When you have worked through the sample, count the number of words you have listed and use Figure 3.3 to obtain the sample's difficulty index.

Figure 3.3. The Mugford readability chart: repetition section
© Leonard Mugford 1970

Number of different words	Word length score																	
	0	1	2	3	4	5	6	7	8	9	10	11	12	13	14	15	16	17
1–18	5.5	5.6	5.7	5.8	6.0	6.1	6.2	6.4	6.5	6.6	6.7	6.8	6.8	6.9	7.0	7.0	7.1	7.1
19–21	5.6	5.7	5.8	6.0	6.1	6.2	6.3	6.4	6.5	6.6	6.7	6.8	6.9	6.9	7.0	7.1	7.1	7.1
22–24	5.7	5.8	5.9	6.1	6.2	6.3	6.4	6.5	6.6	6.7	6.7	6.8	6.9	6.9	7.0	7.1	7.1	7.2
25–27	5.8	6.0	6.1	6.2	6.3	6.4	6.5	6.5	6.6	6.7	6.8	6.8	6.9	7.0	7.0	7.1	7.1	7.2
28–30	6.0	6.1	6.2	6.3	6.4	6.5	6.5	6.6	6.7	6.7	6.8	6.9	7.0	7.0	7.0	7.1	7.1	7.2
31–33	6.1	6.2	6.3	6.4	6.5	6.5	6.6	6.7	6.7	6.8	6.8	6.9	7.0	7.0	7.0	7.1	7.1	7.2
34–36	6.3	6.4	6.4	6.5	6.6	6.6	6.7	6.7	6.8	6.8	6.9	6.9	7.0	7.0	7.1	7.1	7.1	7.2
37–39	6.4	6.5	6.5	6.6	6.7	6.7	6.8	6.8	6.8	6.9	6.9	7.0	7.0	7.0	7.1	7.1	7.1	7.2
40–42	6.6	6.7	6.6	6.7	6.8	6.8	6.8	6.9	6.9	6.9	7.0	7.0	7.0	7.1	7.1	7.1	7.1	7.2
43–45	6.8	6.8	6.8	6.8	6.8	6.9	6.9	6.9	7.0	7.0	7.0	7.0	7.1	7.1	7.1	7.1	7.2	7.2
46–48	6.9	6.9	6.9	6.9	6.9	7.0	7.0	7.0	7.0	7.0	7.0	7.1	7.1	7.1	7.1	7.1	7.2	7.2
49–51	7.0	7.0	7.0	7.0	7.0	7.0	7.0	7.0	7.0	7.1	7.1	7.1	7.1	7.1	7.1	7.1	7.2	7.2

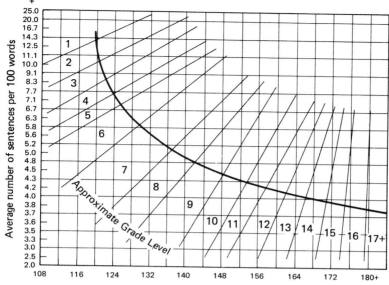

Figure 3.4. Fry's extended readability graph

The Fry graph (1977; Figure 3.4)

This is one of the most straightforward ways of obtaining a readability index. The graphical form is helpful for a number of reasons: it saves time on making calculations; it offers visual information when numerical results might give a spurious impression of accuracy; the user of the graph can tell at a glance if a passage is in comparative terms more difficult than average in vocabulary or in sentence length. This final point is not generally realised, but clearly if the curve represents normal texts, points above the line, or towards the top right quadrant, will represent passages with higher than average vocabulary difficulty, while points below the curve, towards the bottom left quadrant, will suggest greater than average sentence length. These are the directions for using the readability graph:

- Randomly select three sample passages and count out exactly 100 words each, beginning with the beginning of a sentence.
- Count the number of sentences in the 100 words, calculating the length of the fraction of the last sentence to the nearest one-tenth.
- Count the total number of syllables in the 100-word passage. If you don't have a hand counter available, an easy way is to simply put a

mark above every syllable over one in each word, then when you get to the end of the passage, count the number of marks and add 100.

- Enter the graph with the average numbers of sentences and syllables; plot a dot where the two lines intersect. The area where the dot is plotted will give you the approximate US grade level. The UK reading level is 5 + US grade.

- If a great deal of variability is found in syllable count or sentence count, putting more samples into the average is desirable.

- When counting syllables for numerals and abbreviations, count one syllable for each symbol. For example, 1945 is four syllables, IRA is three syllables, and & is one syllable.

The Dale–Chall formula (1948)

The Dale-Chall formula, like the Spache formula, uses a word list as a basis for predicting vocabulary difficulty. The Dale list of 3,000 words (Appendix A) was originally derived from research into the words best known to American eight-year-olds. Although a few American words are clearly out of place in the United Kingdom (what is a bobwhite?), in general the list has proved its worth in British research, by counting as familiar those words spelt in the British way which appear in the American spelling on the list (e.g. *colour, color*). The formula, though time-consuming to compute, has shown up well in validation studies, and is as follows:

$$\text{US grade} = (0.1579 \times \text{PERCENT UFMWDS})$$
$$+ (0.0496 \times \text{WDS/SEN})$$
$$+ 3.6365$$

where UFMWDS = unfamiliar words (for definition, see below)

and WDS/SEN = average number of words per sentence

UK reading level = 5 + US grade

In the light of experience gained in applying their formula to passages of various types, and comparing the formula's prediction with the judgments of experts, Dale and Chall came to feel that the formula scores might be slightly underestimating the difficulty of harder materials. They therefore suggested that the formula score should be converted to a 'corrected grade level'. The 'corrected age levels' below represent the Dale and Chall transformation table, but, as usual, 5 has been added to turn the scores into age levels for UK schools.

Dale–Chall formula score	Corrected age levels
4.9 and below	9 and below
5.0–5.9	10–11
6.0–6.9	12–13
7.0–7.9	14–15
8.0–8.9	16–17
9.0–9.9	College
10.0 and above	College graduate

As with the Spache formula, there are a number of rules for deciding what may be regarded as a 'familiar' word.

Common nouns

● Consider familiar all regular plurals and possessives of words on the list. For example, because *boy, girl, church*, and *army* are on the list, *boy's* (possessive), *girls, churches*, and *armies* (regularly formed plurals) are familiar.

● Count irregular plurals as unfamiliar, even if the singular form appears on the list; *oxen* is unfamiliar, although *ox* is on the list. However, when the plural appears as a separate word or is indicated by the ending in parentheses next to the word, it is considered familiar; *goose* and *geese* appear on the list and both are considered familiar.

● Count as unfamiliar a noun that is formed by adding *-er* or *-r* to a noun or verb appearing on the word list (unless this *er* or *r* form is indicated on the list); *burner* is counted as unfamiliar, although *burn* is on the list. *Owner* is considered familiar because it appears on the list as *own(er)*.

Proper nouns

● Names of persons and places are considered familiar. *Japan, Smith*, and so on, are familiar even though they do not appear on the word list.

● Names of organisations, laws, documents, titles of books, movies, and so on generally comprise several words.

(a) When determining the number of words in a sample, count all the words in the name of an organisation and the like. *Chicago Building Association* should be counted three words. *Declaration of Independence* should be counted three words. *Special rule:* When the title of an organisation, law, and so on is used several times within a sample of 100 words, all the words in the title are counted, no matter how many times they are repeated.

(b) For the unfamiliar word count, consider unfamiliar only words which do not appear on the Dale list, except names of persons or places. *Chicago Building Association* is counted one unfamiliar word (*Association*) since *Building* and *Chicago* are familiar. *Declaration of Independence* is counted as two unfamiliar words – as *of* is on the list.

Special rule: When the name of an organization, law, document, and so on is used several times within a sample of 100 words, count it only twice when making the unfamiliar word count. *Security Council*, if repeated more than twice within a 100-word sample, is counted as four unfamiliar words.

Abbreviations

● (a) In counting the words in a sample, an abbreviation is counted as one word. *Y.M.C.A., Nov., a.m.* and *p.m.* are each counted as one word.

(b) In making the unfamiliar word count, an abbreviation is counted as one unfamiliar word only. *Y.M.C.A.* is considered one unfamiliar word. *Nov.* is considered familiar because the names of the months are on the word list. *U.S., a.m.* and *p.m.* are each considered familiar. *Special rule:* An abbreviation which is used more than twice within a 100-word sample is counted as two unfamiliar words only. *C.I.O.* is counted two unfamiliar words if repeated five times in a 100-word sample.

Verbs

● Consider familiar the third-person, singular forms (-*s*, or -*ies* from *y*), present-participle forms (-*ing*), past-participle forms (-*n*), and past-tense forms (-*ed*, or -*ied* from -*y*), when these are added to verbs appearing on the list. The same rule applies when a consonant is doubled before adding -*ing* or -*ed*. For example, *ask, asking, asked, dropped* and *dropping* are considered familiar, because *ask* and *drop* appear on the word list.

Adjectives

● Comparatives and superlatives of adjectives appearing on the list are considered familiar. The same rule applies if the consonant is doubled before adding -*er* or -*est*. For example, *longer, prettier*, and *bravest* are familiar because *long, pretty*, and *brave* are on the list; *red, redder*, and *reddest* are all familiar.

● Adjectives formed by adding -*n* to a proper noun are familiar. For example, *American, Austrian*.

● Count as unfamiliar an adjective that is formed by adding -*y* to a word that appears on the list. But consider the word familiar if -*y* appears in parentheses following the word. E.g. *woolly* is unfamiliar although *wool* is on the list; *sandy* is familiar because it appears on the list as *sand(y)*.

Adverbs

● Consider adverbs familiar which are formed by adding -*ly* to a word on the list. (In most cases -*ly* is indicated following the word.) *Soundly* is familiar because *sound* is on the list.

● Count as unfamiliar words which add more than -*ly* or change a letter, like *easily*.

Hyphenated words
- Count the hyphenated words as unfamiliar if either word in the compound does not appear on the word list. When both appear on the list, the word is familiar.

Miscellaneous special cases
- Words formed by adding *-en* to a word on the list (unless the *-en* is listed in parentheses or the word itself appears on the list) are considered unfamiliar; *sharpen* is considered unfamiliar although *sharp* is on the list; *golden* is considered familiar because it appears on the list *gold(en)*.
- Count a word unfamiliar if two or more endings are added to a word on the list; *clippings* is considered unfamiliar, although *clip* is on the list.
- Words on the list to which *-tion, -ation, -ment*, and other suffixes not previously mentioned are added are considered unfamiliar, unless the word with the ending is included on the list; *treatment* is unfamilar although *treat* is on the list; *protection* is unfamiliar although *protect* is on the list; *preparation* is unfamiliar although *prepare* is on the list.
- Numerals like *1947, 18* and so on, are considered familiar.

The Flesch formula (1948)

The Flesch formula is one of the best-known readability measures. The formula uses the same variables as the Powers–Sumner–Kearl formula, but it does not immediately produce a US grade level. Since Flesch was primarily interested in assessing adult reading material, he chose a difficulty index which did not relate to grades, but to a notional comprehension score out of 100. Thus a difficult passage would yield a score of below 50, while a single child's book would approach a score of 100. This is the Flesch formula:

$$\text{Reading ease score} = 206.835$$
$$- (0.846 \times \text{SYLLS}/100\text{w})$$
$$- (1.015 \times \text{WDS}/\text{SEN})$$

where SYLLS/100w = syllables per 100 words
and WDS/SEN = average number of words per sentence

It is theoretically possible to produce reading ease scores outside the range 0–100, but these are rare.

For those who wish to relate the reading ease score to age levels Flesch provided a transformation table which is summarised in the centre column of Figure 3.5. This figure is a nomogram; that is, by using a ruler between the left-hand and right-hand columns of the figure the reader can save the bother

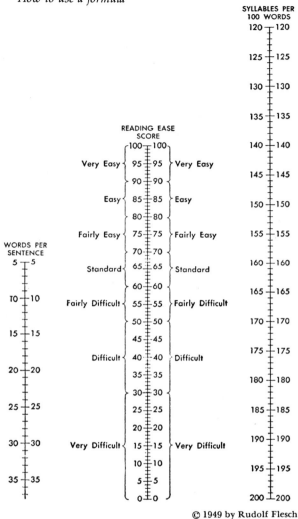

Figure 3.5. Flesch formula nomogram: a sample with 15 words per sentence and 140 syllables per 100 words has a reading ease score of about 73

of calculating the reading ease score by simply noting the point at which the central column is bisected. You can verify the accuracy of the reading ease scores in Table 3.4 by using the nomogram together with the data in Table 3.3.

A more accurate arithmetical transformation of the reading

ease score in terms of school grades may be valuable in certain circumstances. The algorithms given here were obtained from the General Motors STAR computer program which was the basis for the more extensive FORTRAN program reproduced as Appendix C in this book.

Reading ease score (RES)	Flesch grade level (FGL)	Reading level
Over 70	$-((\text{RES} - 150)/10)$	FGL + 5
Over 60	$-((\text{RES} - 110)/5)$	FGL + 5
Over 50	$-((\text{RES} - 93)/3.33)$	FGL + 5
Under 50	$-((\text{RES} - 140)/6.66)$	FGL + 5

Gunning's FOG formula (1952)

This is one of the easiest of all readability indices to work out, and this fact does explain its popularity. Gunning noticed that the vocabulary variable of percentage of polysyllabic words (i.e. words of three or more syllables) was much quicker to count than the total number of syllables in a passage, and since this variable correlated highly with other vocabulary variables, it seemed reasonable to work from it in assessing readability. The problem with this variable is that it does not discriminate very effectively between relatively simple passages of prose, since the percentage of polysyllabic words per 100 words will be uniformly low. The FOG formula (Gunning suggested that the acronym stood for 'frequency of gobbledegook') is as follows:

$$\text{US grade} = 0.4 \times (\text{WDS/SEN} + \% \text{ PSW})$$

where WDS/SEN = average number of words per sentence
and % PSW = percentage of polysyllabic words

$$\text{UK reading level} = \text{US grade} + 5$$

McLaughlin's SMOG formula (1969)

This is the easiest and quickest formula of all to work out by hand, since McLaughlin found an extremely clever way round the time-consuming business of counting every word in every sentence. This formula uses a single variable, the number of polysyllabic (i.e. three-or-more syllable) words in 30 sentences.

This variable focusses on vocabulary, but clearly if the thirty sentences are lengthy, there will be more opportunity to encounter long words, so sentence-length is taken account of indirectly.

The fact that the SMOG formula (described by McLaughlin as a 'simple measure of gobbledegook') contains a square root calculation need not alarm us. Most pocket calculators now carry a square root function, but even so, McLaughlin intended to spare us complex calculations. In his formula the square root is taken from the *nearest perfect square* to the actual number of polysyllabic words found in thirty sentences. Thus if 50 polysyllabic words were found, the calculation would proceed from the nearest perfect square, i.e. 49 (7×7). Similarly, for 31 we should proceed from 36 (6×6), and so on. As mentioned earlier, it is wiser to sample from more than one place in a book, and it would be common to select ten sentences from the beginning, ten from the middle, and ten from the end. McLaughlin's SMOG formula is:

$$\text{US grade} = 3 + \sqrt{P} \quad \text{(i.e. 3 plus the square root of P)}$$

where P = the nearest perfect square to the number of polysyllabic words (i.e. three-or-more syllable words) in thirty sentences

$$\text{UK reading level} = \text{US grade} + 5$$

Finally, it must be noted that McLaughlin stressed that his formula was attempting to predict the grade level necessary for 100% comprehension of a text. This is a very difficult claim to examine or substantiate, but at any rate it would lead us to expect higher difficulty scores than on most formulae, which were originally validated against lower comprehension levels.

The FORCAST formula (Sticht, 1973)

This formula was devised by Tom Sticht and his collaborators on US Army projects. Its orientation is firmly towards functional literacy and not school learning, but Sticht's interests produced the only measure in this chapter which does not include any sentence-length variable. This fact robs the formula of some predictive validity, but it nevertheless can be useful in assessing forms, job materials or other print which is not in normal sentence form, and which could not otherwise be assessed by a formula at all. It uses just one variable: the number of single-syllable words in a 150-word passage. The FORCAST formula is:

$$\text{US grade} = 20 - (\text{NOSW} \div 10)$$

where NOSW = number of one-syllable words in a passage of 150 words

Conclusion

In this chapter information has been offered which will enable you to apply a variety of readability measures to texts. It is vital to bear in mind the caveats about validity and reliability given in the early part of the chapter. These, together with the more detailed comments on applicability and utility which are offered in Chapter 5 will provide a reasonably secure basis for using the measures beneficially in the classroom.

However, before we turn specifically to the use of readability measures in various age and subject groups, it is necessary to examine an entirely different approach to measuring text difficulty which has become increasingly important in recent years. This is the technique known as cloze procedure.

TEXT A. IRON AGE CLOTHING

Sample 1

After many more years, people called Celts came from the sea and brought another metal with them called iron. It made better knives, swords and tools because it was harder than bronze, which was still used for many things such as pins, brooches and bowls.

Twisting wool into long threads is called spinning. This was mostly done by girls.

The stick in the girl's right hand is called the spindle and the round weight on the end is the whorl. On her shoulder is the distaff with a roll of wool. She twists the wool with her fingers until she / has a piece long enough to tie on to the spindle stick, which spins round and twists the wool into thread.   (121 words)

Sample 2

The threads were made into cloth by weaving. You can see in the picture that some threads are fixed down the frame to keep them straight, and the girl weaves her threads in and out across them. In this way they made woollen cloth.

Flax, a plant with a pretty blue flower, grew wild in the woods and fields. The bronze and iron age people found that if they soaked flax plants in the river and dried them in the sun, they could pick out the silky part of the stems and spin it into thread. This was made into/a cloth called linen.   (104 words)

Sample 3

They dyed their linen and woollen clothes with dyes made from plants and tree bark. At first, the bronze age people just wrapped the cloth round themselves and fastened it with pins and brooches. This girl has sewn her dress under the arms and she has a belt with a bronze buckle. Her hair is worn in a net, with long pins. This man wears a short tunic and a woollen cap. His cloak has no sleeves. They both wear skin shoes. The bronze buckles and brooches were beautifully made. Some ornaments were made of gold, which was found in / Britain at this time.   (104 words)

TEXT B. THE NITROGEN PROBLEM

Sample 1

Some seventy years ago, scientists were worried by what was called the 'nitrogen problem'. They discussed the problem at learned gatherings and wrote about it in learned journals. What was this problem and how did it arise? During the nineteenth century, agriculture had made great strides, thanks to better equipment and new farming methods. Chemists had investigated ways of raising the yields of crops and one of them, the German scientist, Justus von Liebig (1803–1873), had paid special attention to the use of fertilizers. Other scientists demonstrated that certain chemicals containing nitrogen, the nitrogenous fertilizers, could double or treble the / yield of grain crops.

(104 words)

Sample 2

This was important because the population of Europe was growing rapidly and it was becoming necessary to grow more wheat to feed the people. Meanwhile the chemical industry was demanding more nitrogen to make dyestuffs and high explosives such as dynamite. Thus agriculture and industry were competing with one another for the available nitrogenous compounds. And seventy years ago nitrogenous compounds were not plentiful. They were obtained, often with difficulty, from different sources. Urine had been used as a source for centuries. Compounds from dung, with a higher nitrogen content, were also used. One of these was potassium nitrate (Saltpetre).   (100 words)

Sample 3

This was imported mainly from India, and being expensive, was kept for the manufacture of black powder and nitric acid. Another was guano, the droppings of sea birds which had accumulated on the islands off Peru. Guano had been shipped to Europe from the beginning of the nineteenth century but by the end of the century, the deposits had been almost worked out. Larger supplies of nitrogen gradually became available from two other sources, both of which are still in use. One was the gas and steel industries. The carbonization of coal to make gas and coke yields a by-product / called ammoniacal water.   (103 words)

4 Cloze procedure as a measure of readability

In this chapter we define cloze procedure, then look at its four areas of use: readability measurement, as a standardised comprehension test, as a diagnostic tool for individual readers, and as an aid to reading development. In looking at readability measurement, we also consider what various percentage cloze scores mean, and we ask what length of passage is needed, what rate of deletion should be used, and how cloze tests should be administered.

What is cloze procedure?

The term *cloze procedure* was first used by the American researcher Wilson Taylor (1953) to describe a new way of testing comprehension. Instead of preparing a series of comprehension questions, the tester simply deleted words from the passage on a regular basis, for example every fifth word. He then used the number of correctly guessed words as an index of how much the reader had understood. Printed below is an example of a cloze passage which we shall discuss later in this chapter. The reader may care to write down on a piece of paper what seem to be the most likely answers, and then compare them with what the author wrote. The author's original words are given at the end of this section.

The _____ may guide themselves by _____ well known stars such _____ the Pole Star, or _____ by the direction and _____ of the wind. They _____ chiefly on other groups _____ their people who are _____ very hospitable and who _____ travellers by giving them _____ best of everything. A _____ will exchange his mount _____ a camp leaving the _____ one as payment for _____ new horse. Every family _____ treat others in this _____ way because they may _____ the same sort of _____ themselves one day. There _____ bound to be more _____ in their lifestyle.

84

In one sense it seems a little bizarre to suggest that a cloze test is measuring the reader's comprehension of a passage: the reader has never seen and probably never does see the original passage in its intact form. What the text examines is the extent to which the reader can predict from the surrounding context the words which the author wrote. While this is different from normal comprehension tests, it is nevertheless a part of normal reading behaviour, as was argued in Chapter 2 when we considered Frank Smith's view of the reading process. Few psychologists now hold to the view that normal reading is a letter-by-letter decoding process; there is too much experimental evidence which points the other way. A fluent reader only sees about 80% of the text he reads in clear focus: the author's message is reconstructed through a mixture of perception and guesswork. One of the things cloze procedure does is to externalise some of the guesswork in a controlled manner.

Of course it is not the case that a normal reader's sampling of the visual input received at the retina is simply based on his skipping every fifth word; the selection process is infinitely more complex. But one of the aspects of performance which differentiates good from poor readers is their capacity to utilise partial information effectively, and in a cloze test this is precisely what the reader must do.

The actual term *cloze* has been considered to be slightly unfortunate by some commentators. Taylor used the term tentatively to indicate a connection with the concept of *closure* in Gestalt psychology. Gestaltists emphasise our tendency to see incomplete figures as complete ones, and to illustrate this Taylor used the example of a broken circle which we 'see' as a whole, by mentally closing up the gaps. He went on to describe what a cloze test subject does in similar terms, stressing that the task is to complete the 'sentence pattern' for each deleted word. Since the term *cloze* was coined, it has caused innumerable typing and printing errors, which in themselves demonstrate Taylor's point. However, a criticism of the concept of closure is mentioned by Weaver (1977b), in a paper originally given in 1965. The Gestalt explanations of closure are primarily related to the subjects' perceptions, and not to conscious thought processes as such. In other words, it is misleading to imply that when subjects complete a cloze test, they are supplying the missing word on the same basis on which they would mentally close up an incomplete geometrical shape. Weaver asserted that there was absolutely no experimental evidence to support the view that readers fill in cloze deletions in this way. His own research (Weaver, 1963) suggested that the crucial aptitude in answering cloze tests is *redundancy utilisation*.

Here, *redundancy* is a technical term which describes the features of a message which allow us to reconstruct lost or ambiguous fragments. For example, the message *All hands on deck* contains a high degree of redundancy: provided they were assured that there was no trick answer, most fluent readers could reconstruct the whole message if they were presented with any three of the four words. The sentence *Lungworts have dimorphic flowers*, on the other hand, contains very little redundancy: although *have* could be predicted from the other three words, any other deletion would be extremely difficult to replace correctly without additional contextual clues. Nevertheless, a reader who could use such clues to good effect would be at an advantage, and it is this ability that Weaver had in mind when he used the term *redundancy utilisation*.

Cloze procedure involves asking the reader to fill in gaps, but in many respects it is very different from other 'gap-filling' exercises. As Taylor's original article clearly showed, the early studies of cloze procedure were done by researchers with an interest in communication theory and the mathematical measurement of information in a transmitted message. In the field of communications, the amount of information a message contains can be described in terms of how predictable it is. We know, for example, how predictable occurrences of individual letters are, taken singly or in groups. If you close your eyes and mark a point on this page with a pencil, the chances are that you will hit a blank space, since there are more of these than any single letter. If your point has touched a letter, the greatest likelihood is that it will be the letter *e*, and there is a gradually diminishing probability for all the other letters. But in a language, letters are not put next to each other in a random sequence, and we can also describe the set of probabilities related to the chances of finding one letter succeeding another. Thus *q* is generally followed by *u*, but *b* is never followed by *x*.

The chance of one pair of letters occurring together is called their *transitional probability*, and this concept of transitional probabilities can be applied to sequences of words as well as letters. In everyday communication we use a relatively small set of words and many highly predictable utterances. Telegraph companies realised this decades ago, and stopped transmitting messages such as HAPPY ANNIVERSARY or HAPPY BIRTHDAY in full, in order to make more efficient use of their equipment. These messages had a high degree of redundancy and a low amount of information. By the same token, if there was a typing error or electrical interference during transmission of an unabbreviated message, the person receiving it could reconstruct the intended message if what was received was HAPPY ANNHAUCIRAR. In a cloze test the reader is in the position of a radio ham whose set fails to receive certain signals which the source (an author) has tried to transmit. He has most of the message available, and two factors will determine how successful he is at reconstructing the message. The first is his redundancy utilisation, i.e. his ability to use his awareness of linguistic conventions, vocabulary and so on; the second is the information load of the message itself. The key point here is that this second factor is a feature of the message, not of the reader. The transitional probabilities between words in sentences from a botanical textbook are lower than those in spoken discourse; the transitional probabilities between words in a poem are generally much lower than those in a short story. In the case of the textbook and the poem these lower probabilities will make the words harder to predict, and this is precisely what we examine when cloze procedure is used as a measure of readability. What we examine is the average predictability of the words in the passage under review, and the lower the percentage of words correctly guessed, the harder the passage.

The answers to the cloze test at the start of this section are: *Kazaks, watching, as, even, feel, rely, of, always, help, the, Kazak, at, first, the, will, trusting, need, help, are, changes*. Multiply by five to obtain a percentage score.

The four uses of cloze procedure

Although Taylor had a single and specific purpose in mind when he introduced the term, cloze procedure has been developed in four general directions, and although our central focus is on readability work, it is worth outlining briefly all four before developing the readability aspect.

The four uses are:

(a) readability measurement
(b) standardised comprehension testing
(c) diagnosis of individual readers' abilities or deficiencies
(d) reading development

We shall consider each of these in turn.

Readability measurement

In a lucid and penetrating review article, Klare, Sinaiko and Stolurow (1972) remind us that unlike formulae, cloze tests can measure but not predict readability, so there is a generic difference between cloze procedure and the types of readability tests discussed in Chapter 3. In another important paper, Lawrence Miller (1975) draws out three crucial differences between cloze and multiple-choice comprehension tests (on which readability formulae were generally validated). First, cloze procedure measures the difficulty of the passage itself, not the difficulty of the questions which are set on it. In a multiple-choice test, the questions may be more difficult than the passage itself, or may even fail to examine the reader's understanding at all. Secondly, a cloze test measures what a reader brings to the passage in terms of content knowledge. By contrast, in a multiple-choice test the questions come after a reader has read the passage, and it is difficult to know whether the examinee got an answer correct because he knew it beforehand, or because he had learned it by reading the passage carefully. Thirdly, if each of the possible versions of a cloze test is used (for example, if we were deleting every fifth word, one passage would begin deletions on word one, another on word two, and so on until all five possible versions had been produced), the test measures the difficulty of every single word, phrase and sentence in the entire passage. In a multiple-choice comprehension test on the other hand, it is impossible to be anywhere near so detailed; the items are a tiny and sometimes ill-assorted subset of the possible items which could be written, and the questions cannot be so precise as cloze procedure in their measurement of between-sentence meanings and relationships.

The stability of cloze procedure as an instrument for testing reading comprehension seemed to make it ideal for readability analysis, and during the mid-1960s a note of euphoria crept into some research reports based on cloze work. John Bormuth (1966) wrote: 'the development of the cloze test solved the problem of validly measuring difficulty while it simultaneously provided additional power and flexibility in making those measurements'. In this paper and a subsequent extensive research report (Bormuth, 1969a), he made out the case for a new approach to readability measurement based on cloze procedure on the one hand and 'new' variables drawn from contemporary work in linguistics on the other.

In order to use cloze scores as indices of comparative passage difficulty, what a researcher normally does is to ask the same group of children to complete cloze tests on a number of passages. He then takes the mean percentage of correctly predicted words as an index of difficulty. These percentages can be compared, with the lowest percentage indicating the hardest passage and the highest indicating the easiest.

Later in this chapter in the section on how to use cloze for readability measurement in the classroom, we shall discuss such issues as what rate of deletions to use, whether there should be fixed-length gaps or ones which are proportional to the length of the omitted word, and how many children are needed for reliable results.

Significance of the cloze score. What exactly does a cloze score mean? If a class gets on average a certain score, for example 40% correct responses on a cloze test, does it suggest they have understood it, or should the score be much higher if we are to conclude that the passage is readable? Is there a percentage figure which can be used as a criterion for comprehension regardless of the kind of passage in use or the overall ability of the reader? If this were so, it would be extremely helpful, because we could then use the figure as a yardstick in classroom estimates of text difficulty with every kind of group. Although there is no single answer to this latter question, work has been done which has provided us with useful reference points in interpreting cloze scores. Two different approaches have been adopted, one comparing cloze scores with multiple-choice comprehension test scores, and the other using an information gain score as a criterion. These two approaches have yielded slightly different results, but they are not irreconcilable.

In a useful paper, Rankin and Culhane (1969) summarised much of the important work which has been done in searching for a percentage cloze score which was consistent with an adequate level of comprehension on the part of a reader who was taking a multiple-choice test. Bormuth (1968) has also contributed some useful research.

As we observed in Chapter 2, the notion of 75% and 90% correct answers on comprehension tests has proved a useful one for American teachers. They have used the figures as a rule-of-thumb to describe the so-called *instructional* and *independent* levels at which texts are used. What this means is that a passage on which a child can answer 75% of questions correctly is at his instructional level, i.e. he is probably gaining enough from it for the text to be profitably employed in the classroom provided the teacher's help is available. By contrast, for a child to be able to work independently from a text there must be greater comprehension, and thus a figure of 90% correct answers on a comprehension test is used as a criterion for reading at the independent level. There was fairly close agreement between the two studies with regard to the percentage cloze scores which were comparable to these levels. At the instructional level (75% correct on multiple choice) the children's cloze scores obtained by Bormuth, and Rankin and Culhane were 44% and 41% respectively. We can interpret this cautiously by saying that a cloze score of 40%–45% seems to indicate an acceptable level of comprehension, provided that a teacher's help is readily available. At the independent level (90% correct on multiple-choice tests) the criterion cloze scores are naturally rather higher: 57% and 61%. Again, being cautious we could say that a cloze score of about 60% corresponds to this more stringent comprehension criterion. In other words, for a group to be able to work successfully on a book on their own, they should be capable of scoring 60% on a fifth-word deletion cloze test based on it. The phrase 'a group' is used here in preference to 'a reader' because one could not necessarily make the assumption that each individual reader who does not score 60% or more is not understanding the passage adequately. Cloze test scores, like every other test score, will include some degree of inaccuracy, and therefore in assessing readability grouped scores are likely to be more reliable than the scores of individuals.

The second method of deriving a percentage cloze score which we can use as a reference point in readability work is based on the concept of *information gain*. This concept was introduced in Chapter 2 with reference to the procedure of subtracting readers' comprehension test scores which had been attained *without* seeing the passage from their scores on the same test *after* they had seen the passage. The difference between their scores under the 'passage out' and 'passage in' conditions shows how much new learning has taken place, and this is the information gain score. In a very interesting experiment, Bormuth (1969b) set out to explore the relationship between this type of information gain score and cloze test results. His aim was to see whether he could pinpoint a percentage cloze score which was consistent with a significant rise in the information a reader gained from a passage. What he did was to pair his subjects on the basis of a pre-test of the cloze type, so that he had readers of approximately equal ability in each pairing. We can call the subjects in each pairing X and Y, which will make Figure 4.1 a little easier to interpret. He next gave X a cloze test on a passage and Y an information gain test, and for each pair he was able to plot one point on the graph. He then used some mathematical procedures for smoothing out the curve and ended up with the graph which is reproduced as Figure 4.1.

What Bormuth concluded from the results of this study was that at approximately the level of 38% correct cloze items there was a noticeable increase in information gain scores. As may be seen from the graph itself, the rate of increase (the slope of the graph) also decreases sharply above that point, and the cloze scores increase without much of a corresponding increase in information gain score. As we have stressed elsewhere, gain scores are notoriously difficult to handle, and it could be that when a good reader takes the information gain test he does so well without the passage because of his general knowledge, linguistic competence and general intelligence, that he cannot gain a great deal on the follow-up test with the passage available. Bormuth himself stressed that this was only a pre-

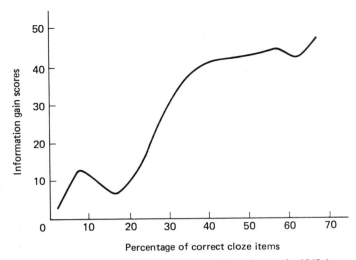

Figure 4.1. Cloze scores and information gain (from Bormuth, 1969a)

liminary study, but even so it is quite widely known, and Bormuth's 38% figure is better known in the United Kingdom than the percentages based on multiple-choice criteria.

To sum up, Bormuth's 38% criterion drawn from the information gain study seems sufficiently close to the 40%–45% figures derived from multiple-choice tests for us to be able to retain the latter as an indicator of adequate comprehension for texts in use at the instructional level. For determining the adequacy of comprehension for texts used at the independent level, the figure of 60% correct cloze items would seem to be the most useful one.

Verbatim versus synonym scoring. Broadly speaking, when cloze test scores are being used as indices of readability, it is important to accept as correct only the exact words which the author wrote. These are normally termed *verbatim* responses. Thus, in the sentence *The men and women will earn wages on* [   ] *state farms*, only the word *collective* can be regarded as an acceptable answer. Minor misspellings are acceptable, but another word which might be grammatically correct, and which might seem a reasonably close synonym, such as *communal*, is to be regarded as incorrect. Why is this?

The main reason for preferring verbatim scoring is essentially practical: synonym scoring takes much longer than verbatim scoring and it may be less reliable. Imagine a researcher who is interested in looking at cloze scores on a number of passages. For greater reliability, he is almost certainly adopting an 'all-version' test, i.e. all five versions if fifth-word deletion is used, so that scores are obtained for every word in every passage. If he decides to use synonym scoring, then, in order to have the tests scored reliably, he must decide in advance what synonyms are acceptable, and he must do this for every word in every passage. In the early days of cloze research a number of studies were conducted to consider the results of verbatim versus synonym scoring, and the most important point to note is that experimenters (e.g. Bormuth, 1965a) found extremely high correlations between the two scoring systems. This means that for readability measurement little is gained by going to the enormous trouble of accepting synonyms; a similar set of results is obtained if a verbatim scoring system is used.

Standardised comprehension testing

Cloze tests can be used in the same manner as other group tests of reading, whose purpose is to give a general indication of the overall level of reading attainment. The best-known tests have been the Gap (McLeod, 1970) and Gapadol (McLeod and Anderson, 1973) tests, and although their geneology is not as impressive as that of reading tests which were given to large UK samples of children in order to provide norms, both tests have two useful attributes. They are very easy to administer, and very quick to mark. Figure 4.2 reproduces a part of the Gap test, and it demonstrates the decreasing print sizes which the reader encounters as he progresses through the test. The Gap test takes fifteen minutes to complete, and the Gapadol test half an hour. Both tests take about two minutes to mark.

In contrast, some reading tests currently used as large-scale screening devices have a twenty-minute pre-test followed by two half-hour main tests, and take half an hour to mark. A long test with a number of subsections may serve a useful purpose in fine-grain diagnostic testing, but unless its results are going to be used on an individual basis it may well be a waste of resources to give such a test to thousands of children. If the aim

After you have stirred . . . . for a time, it

seems to . . . . disappeared. Of course

it is in the tea. . . . . can taste it. But you

cannot find . . . .

Long   ago   in   the   land   of   Sweden   there   was

. . . . little girl who sang. She sang with the

. . . . as they chirped in the hedges. She

. . . . with   the   wind   as   it   sighed   in

. . . . trees.   She   sang   in   time   with

. . . . own footsteps as she skipped along the

country lanes.

Figure 4.2. A reproduction of a section of the Gap reading test

is to establish early on in the school year which children are poor
readers, it might be preferable to use a short test as a screening
measure, and then to follow up with more-specific diagnostic
testing for the bottom 40%, beginning with the children who
obtained the lowest scores on the screening test. As we have
noted already, it is very easy to construct a new cloze test, and
there is no problem of writing and piloting dozens of test items
in order to ensure that the test is doing a similar job to other

cloze tests. In other words, for a screening exercise in school it is perfectly reasonable to construct one's own test. It would be as well to choose four or five passages of increasing difficulty, in order to ensure that poor readers get at least some right and that good readers are stretched, but this should not be too onerous. Constructing one's own cloze test takes some time, but it saves money, avoids administration and possible delay associated with official orders, and does ensure that the test is not one which any children have met previously.

The National Foundation for Educational Research (NFER) has developed cloze tests which can be used for 'norm-referenced' purposes, that is to make comparisons with the attainment of other groups of children of a similar age. These are called *reading level tests*, (NFER, 1977) and as the name implies, the passages are written at a variety of levels of difficulty, so the tests are more discriminating than the Gap and Gapadol tests, particularly at the extremes of the ability range.

Diagnosis of individual readers' abilities or deficiencies

We made the point above that one of the key competences examined by cloze procedure is the reader's redundancy utilisation, i.e. his ability to use the information surrounding a deletion as a basis for correctly predicting the missing word. It is possible to learn a good deal about an individual reader's attempts to interrogate the text and reconstruct its meaning from the answers which he offers. Consider this section from an attempt by twelve-year-old Richard at a tenth-word deletion version of a passage. His answers are in italic.

They rely chiefly on other groups of their people who are always very hospitable and who *are* travellers by giving them the best of everything. A *money* will exchange his mount at a camp leaving the *number* one as payment for the new horse. Every family *has* treat others in this trusting way because they may *be* the same sort of help themselves one day. There *is* bound to be more and more changes in the   of the Kazaks. The group of families known as   clan is likely to find itself settled in a *near* village. The men and women will earn wages on   state farms and spend their money on clothing and *food* goods made in factories far away. More men will *go* in the coalmines and steelworks which are developing rapidly *in* Kazakstan. The children will go to school and learn *about* books instead of just by copying their elders. Although *they* belonged to a form of the Moslem religion their *own* spirits have stopped them following the laws very closely. *By* probably will not bother too much that religion is *in* encouraged in the Soviet Union. As long as they *do* not parted from their beloved horses the Kazaks will *live* happy enough.

One conclusion which can be drawn from an analysis of Richard's errors is that he does not appear to be utilising the information which follows a gap as an additional basis for deciding on the missing word; at least, he does not appear to take account of information beyond the phrase boundary following the gap. Thus, in the first sentence printed, Richard's word *are* is acceptable within the context of *and who are travellers*, but it is incompatible with the succeeding phrase which explains in general terms what the Kazaks do, and which clearly suggests the need for a transitive verb rather than the copula.

The ability to use the information beyond the gap in cloze tests is very important, and its significance goes beyond this one test procedure. In an interesting experiment, Mary Neville and Tony Pugh (1976–77) showed that it was a major difference between good and poor readers. Neville and Pugh gave children a normal cloze test, and then followed up with one of two special versions of cloze procedure, in which the children were only given the passage up to each gap, but not beyond it. One of these special presentations was a tape-recorded version, and the other was a small booklet, but in each case the effect was that the reader did not have access to the passage beyond each deletion; the passage was presented a section at a time, and the child had to answer before he went on to the next item, and could not go back to correct answers later. For good readers, the effect of these restricted presentations was dramatic: their scores dropped by about 30% compared with the full cloze test. In contrast, the scores of the poor readers were not depressed at all by the loss of information beyond each gap. In fact, although their scores were generally much lower than those of the good readers, many poor readers showed a small improvement under the listening condition, and did slightly better than when they had to cope with a full cloze test. No doubt this was because they were spared problems of decoding and word recognition in having the text read for them. Nevertheless the fact remains that the poor readers' scores on the full cloze test were not enhanced by the opportunity to use the 'backward acting' clues of the text which followed each gap, and this may suggest an area for remedial attention, on an individual or a group basis.

As yet, the use of cloze procedure as a clinical technique is relatively unexplored, but the Open University courses on reading development have provided an important initial impetus to such work. The BBC's handbook which accompanied the radio series 'Reading after ten' (Longley, 1977) includes a section in which Elizabeth Goodacre discusses the use of cloze procedure for diagnostic purposes, and reprints an example of a cloze passage which was tackled by a poor reader. No doubt future work in this field will include a more systematic examination of errors made by good and poor readers, along the lines used by Neville and Pugh. They differentiated between syntactic, semantic and morphological appropriateness of answers as well as considering whether the child had access to 'backward acting' clues. When further work along these lines is supplemented by a developmental analysis, so that changes in children's silent reading strategies at different age levels are understood more fully, it seems likely that cloze procedure will become an even more valuable diagnostic tool.

Reading development

Cloze procedure has been used as an aid to reading development since the early 1960s. Much of the literature on these early studies is comparatively difficult to obtain, but fortunately an excellent review by Eugene Jongsma (1971) summarises work done up to 1970. Jongsma noted an interesting shift in the pattern of experimental studies reported during the 1960s. Up to 1967, many researchers hypothesised that giving children lots of practice in cloze tests would increase their awareness of the value of contextual information, and they therefore gave practice in cloze tests and then looked for gains in overall reading comprehension. This type of study was conducted on good readers, poor readers, college students and second-language English speakers. The results were uniformly depressing: doing cloze exercises did not in itself produce any significant gains in reading ability.

The study which reversed this trend was a doctoral thesis written by Ruby Martin of Syracuse University in 1968 which Jongsma summarises. In Martin's study a nine-week programme of cloze exercises produced significant gains in silent reading ability, and she attributed this to one crucial fact: the cloze tests involved discussion. Martin's subjects were college freshmen, and as a part of the cloze training, they were encouraged to verbalise the reasons why they had chosen a particular word, and these were discussed in the group. Amazing as it may seem, this was a novel teaching technique. Previous studies had begun from the implicit assumption that doing cloze exercises alone would enhance reading ability, but this appears not to be the case. Earlier, Richard Bloomer's extensive study (Bloomer, 1966) of 'non-overt reinforced cloze procedure' had suggested that this was the problem. Bloomer gave over 1,000 children various types of cloze exercise, but he offered no overt reinforcement, i.e. there was no discussion, and no feedback for the child to indicate whether he was guessing correctly or not. In the conclusion of his report, Bloomer acknowledges that more reinforcement would perhaps have made the cloze exercises more valuable, and subsequent work has tended to support this view.

In a more recent study, Dolores Kennedy and Paul Weener (1973) demonstrated significant gains in reading and listening comprehension among eight-year-old children who had five twenty-minute lessons of cloze exercises which included a carefully controlled correction procedure. Kennedy and Weener concluded that their procedure caused students to pay attention to units larger than a single word, and although they warned that further research is required to determine specifically what perceptual and attentional processes were being influenced by the training, they did feel that their results implied a role for cloze procedure in reading development.

In the United Kingdom, Christopher Walker's book on reading development (Walker, 1974) suggests that small group cloze exercises are valuable, and he offers examples of possible approaches in the classroom. The Schools Council Effective Use of Reading project began an evaluation of the potential of group cloze exercises in a number of subject areas, and the continuation project Reading for Learning in the Secondary School is extending and developing this work. It seems clear from research findings already available that a small group context for cloze exercises is best if the teacher's aim is reading development rather than some form of test. Individual cloze tests may be valuable for readability measurement or measuring reading attainment, but without some kind of feedback or reinforcement, they do not seem to aid reading development. English teachers cannot but reflect on the possible generalisability of this finding. Many of the comprehension exercises which teachers think of as the cornerstone of the children's reading development have very little reinforcement built into them, and if feedback is given, it may be delayed by a week or more. Such exercises may assist in confirming the level of a child's reading ability, but it is doubtful whether they are assisting his reading development.

Using cloze tests in the classroom

In this section we shall consider some of the important practical and administrative aspects of using cloze procedure as a readability measure in the classroom. It must be accepted that cloze testing involves a good deal more administration than does calculating a formula score, but if the technique is used effectively it can provide certain information which a formula cannot. Cloze scores are sensitive to the variations within a specific target group in a way that a formula cannot be. One such source of variation might be a group's background knowledge of the subject-matter of the test. Another possible source is the overall level of linguistic competence of the group, should it differ from the norm in some way. Furthermore, unlike most readability formulae, cloze tests are not 'fooled' by syntactically simple long sentences or by short but unfamiliar words. The appropriate time to use cloze procedure, therefore, is if it is important to know how well a specific group or groups can comprehend a book, or if the validity of using a readability formula is in doubt.

Before offering specific suggestions about constructing and administering cloze tests it is necessary to recapitulate on one concept which is important in any readability work – reliability. As in the case of formulae computation, there are two types of reliability to be considered, one related to possible variations of difficulty within the book from one section to another, and the other related to whether the test scores which are produced on a specific passage are reliable.

The first issue is relatively straightforward. Sampling reliability can be increased by choosing three extracts from different places in the book and then combining the results into one overall percentage correct score; this is essentially similar to the procedure of taking a number of samples when a formula is being used, although it must be said that we know comparatively little of the actual variation of cloze scores between extracts from different sections of a book. In a study carried out for the Transport and Road Research Laboratory (Harrison, 1977b) into the readability of road-user literature, I looked at the variation in mean cloze scores on two groups of four passages, each group being taken from a single long booklet. In the case of one group of passages, the difference between the highest and lowest cloze scores was 5.3%, and in the case of the other group it was 4.4%. This amount of variation was not large, and it suggested that for certain types of passage at least sampling adequacy may be less of a problem than it is when one is working with formula scores.

In general, though, this is not an aspect of cloze measurement which has been given much attention, and the recommendation that 'at least two samples per section' should be taken, which Klare has made (Klare *et al.*, 1972), appears to be pragmatic and based on the need for caution rather than on specific analysis of sampling adequacy in cloze testing.

The second aspect of reliability to consider is that related to the accuracy of the percentage cloze scores derived from a particular group of readers. Did an adequate number of students (i.e. not less than 30) take part in the test, to ensure that the results did not contain too much random variation? How many blanks were there? Can we say how many deletions are necessary to produce a reliable cloze score? The answer is that we can, in broad terms: in order to avoid effects which are due to random variation (such as might come from beginning a sequence of deletions on the fourth word of the passage rather than the third) it is reckoned necessary to have at least 35 deletions. Better still, in order to allow a margin of error, between 40 and 50 deletions may be considered adequate in classroom work. But decisions about the number of subjects and number of deletions on text passages are not independent: if the number of children who take a cloze test is increased this will itself increase the reliability of the test, and consequently fewer items will be needed. In an interesting paper aimed at a research rather than a classroom audience, Bormuth (1965b) demonstrated that reliability is increased more by adding a given number of items than by adding the same number of subjects. He also argued that this was slightly more economical in total subject time. Against this was the point that increasing the number of items would result in longer and therefore more expensive tests, so the final decision would have to be based on a balance of statistical, administrative and economic factors.

How should the test passages be selected?

Unless the text is too brief to permit it, passages should be chosen at random from the book to be analysed. Three passages are generally reckoned to be enough, and these should not begin in the middle of a paragraph. Many teachers prefer to offer a brief lead into the test before deletions commence, and although there is little or no empirical evidence to support this in terms of increased scores, it does make some subjects feel less insecure with a difficult text. The total length of the passage or passages used will vary according to the number of deletions made and the rate of deletions used. To obtain the minimum number of deletions which is needed for a reasonably reliable one-version cloze test, which is 35, a text of about 180 words is needed on fifth-word deletion. For seventh-word deletion, a 250-word text is required. A total of 50 deletions would increase reliability, and this would require passages of 250 and 350 words for fifth-word and seventh-word deletions respectively.

What rate of deletion should be used?

Fifth-word deletion has been the most widely used rate in the research field, but it is not necessarily the best for the classroom. Fifth-word deletion is attractive for the researcher because it is cheaper: he obtains more items per printed page. If a researcher wishes to use all n versions of an nth word deletion cloze test it is also judicious to obtain as many responses for each separate version as possible in order to increase the reliability of the results, and he can achieve this by keeping n as small as possible. It has been shown by Walter MacGinitie (1961) that once the deletion rate falls below five a cloze test becomes increasingly difficult because the amount of contextual information available is too low to allow the normal process of redundancy utilisation to occur. There is also evidence to suggest that once the rate rises above seven the reader does not gain by being shown increasingly longer stretches of running text between deletions. This fact raises the important issues of the extent to which we can claim that cloze procedure is encouraging or requiring close reading at much beyond the phrase level. If higher deletion rates do not produce better cloze scores, this suggests that the additional text made available to the reader is not particularly informative, that is, it does not convey additional information which is useful in completing the test more successfully.

Between fifth-word and seventh-word deletion experimental results are less clear. Some experiments have suggested that it is useful to the student to make available the additional information which comes from seventh-word deletion, but results have varied between different subject areas. Klare and his collaborators (Klare *et al.*, 1972) have suggested that seventh-word rather than fifth-word deletion is preferable if the readers are comparatively weak or the passage is likely to be found difficult, and this seems a sound recommendation.

What size should blanks be?

Normally in constructing cloze tests one would try to use a standard length of blank each time a word is omitted. The space commonly left is twelve letter-spaces, and depending on the size of type in use this would amount to approximately 3 cm or 1.2 inches. It would alter the character of the test to give blanks which were proportional in length to the omitted word, since the reader would then have access to additional information which would allow him to exclude a number of alternative possibilities. For a good reader, at least, this would tend to produce higher scores, and it would make comparisons with the 44% and 57% norms difficult, since these were derived from tests which used standard-length blanks.

How should the cloze test be administered?

Four crucial points to make clear to the children who are tackling a cloze readability test are (i) it is important to make an attempt at every blank if at all possible, (ii) only *one* word must be put in each blank, (iii) spelling errors will not be marked wrong if it is clear which word was intended, and (iv) the intention here is not to test the child himself, but rather the difficulty of the passage.

For the teacher there are two possible problems. First, the cloze test should ideally be untimed, and children should be encouraged to work at the test until they have completed as many blanks as they can. Since they are certain to differ in the time they take to do this, it may be advisable to have another activity planned for those who finish first. Secondly, because of the nature of the test, unless children have accepted the teacher's assurances they may be tempted to copy each other's answers, thus totally invalidating the whole exercise. It is important therefore to be clear and convincing in the initial explanation to the groups about the nature of the task, and to be vigilant during its completion.

How should cloze readability tests be scored?

As we have already argued, verbatim (exact word) scoring is essential in readability work. It is faster, more reliable and arguably more valid than synonym scoring. Misspellings should be scored as correct, provided that no change in meaning or ambiguity is introduced. To clarify these points, we can consider the following sentence: *The **diseases** was brought from India, **were** it had killed whole **familys**.* In this sentence the three original words omitted were *disease, where,* and *families*. In scoring the cloze responses we should count *diseases* as wrong, because it incorrectly makes the noun a plural, which represents a change in meaning; *were* is more difficult, but it seems likely to be a misspelling for *where* rather than a verb, and should thus be scored as correct; *familys* is also a misspelling and should be scored as correct.

Interpreting the percentage correct cloze score

The average cloze scores on two passages will give an indication of their relative difficulty, but a teacher will generally wish to know more than simply whether one passage is more difficult than another: he needs to know whether the children in a specific class or group will be able to use the text in their own lessons. For this reason it is very valuable to know what sort of percentage figure is consistent with adequate comprehension.

As we have explained above, three criteria have tended to be used. Bormuth found that a cloze score of 38% was associated with a reasonable level of information gain. On the basis of other experiments he suggested the figures of 44% and 57% as representing respectively instructional and independent levels of reading. Rankin and Culhane replicated Bormuth's 1968 work, and they favoured scores of 41% and 61% for the instructional and independent levels. Broadly speaking, therefore, we can consider scores in relation to these three criterion bands: 35%–40%, 40%–45%, and 55%–60%.

It would appear that the 35%–40% criterion might be too low; Bormuth himself suggests this and he quotes readers as voicing 'strong objections' and exhibiting 'signs of frustration and inattention' when faced by texts on which cloze scores were as low as 35%. This would appear to be an important point for teachers to note, particularly in the light of some of the low scores encountered in school-based work represented later in this chapter. Nevertheless, it must be accepted that the research into cloze criterion scores has not been extensive. In the report referred to above, Bormuth admitted that 'the present state of the art of criterion selection is quite primitive'.

One aspect of this subject which has only recently been explored is the possible difference in cloze responses for texts from different subject areas. In an interesting short study, Judith Cohen, an American researcher, investigated the cloze scores of a group of 60 above-average twelve- and thirteen-year-old readers (Cohen, 1975). The children were all in seventh grade, and the passages chosen for the cloze tests were from narrative fiction ('literature'), social studies textbooks and science textbooks commonly used at seventh grade level. The texts all had comparable scores on the Dale–Chall readability formula. Cohen's main finding was that there were statistically significant differences between cloze scores on passages from different subject areas. The mean scores were 30.5% for literature, 39.6% for social studies and 37.0% for science. All these scores are below the instructional level criteria of either Bormuth or Rankin, and this is doubly surprising because the children were on average one year ahead of national norms in reading ability.

Cohen concluded that 'reading content material poses special problems for students that seem to increase the difficulty of performing on cloze tests'. This conclusion might be criticised as appearing a little bland, but it is preceded by some interesting speculation on the causes of the low scores, particularly those in literature. One possibility is that the linguistic structures of the language of other school textbooks are more complex and various than those in the measured prose of reading test passages. It may also be the case, argues Cohen, that the type of information given in textbooks is intellectually demanding in a different way from that which is included in reading tests. In addition, we could suggest that a 'background knowledge' factor might be more important in school textbooks than in most reading tests, whose aim is to be in a sense 'content free'. Also related to this factor is the issue of motivation, which might vary from one cloze passage to another in a way which would not usually be the case with a formal reading test. Each of these factors could affect cloze scores adversely, or at best could introduce variability into the testing which would lower correlations with the criterion variable (in this case a multiple-choice comprehension test).

Cohen's results seem to suggest that either the schoolbooks in use were much too difficult, or that cloze criterion scores of 44% or 60% are inappropriate for classroom use, since too few books will approach them. Reviewing the arguments, and considering Bormuth's point about the need to avoid making difficulties for readers with poor motivation, it does seem important to retain the 40%–45% score range as indicating that a text is suitable for study at the instructional level. If any texts are used on which children have scored below 40%, then the teacher should bear in mind that most readers will not learn much from the book without a great deal of specific help.

As for the more stringent independent level criteria of 57% for Bormuth and 61% for Rankin and Culhane, one is forced to predict that they will be reached on few school textbooks. In two independent studies I investigated in one case 39 and in another 8 passages drawn from school texts and government documents, and in only one case did a passage produce a mean score of over 57%. Here again the readers were above average, so it would appear that high cloze scores on school textbooks are going to be rather rare, and while it might be premature to dismiss the 60% criterion from our minds, it seems likely that until more work is done the 40%–45% criterion will be the most valuable in the classroom.

Conclusion

In his wide-ranging review of verbal learning, J. B. Carroll (1971, pp. 101–4) raised a number of problems concerning aspects of cloze procedure about which our knowledge was deficient. For the present purpose, the three most important questions were:

(i) How valid is cloze technique?
(ii) How do cloze scores interact with the characteristics of readers?
(iii) How *practical* will it be to use cloze as a readability measure in the classroom?

The first question is a reasonable one. Cloze procedure correlates highly with formal reading tests. In this sense it has a high validity; it measures many of the same aspects of difficulty as a normal comprehension test, and it does so in a systematic and regular manner. Nevertheless cloze procedure is an unusual test of comprehension in that readers never see the original passage intact. Furthermore, they are never required to comment on, explain or recall any of the test passage, which would be normal in a test of reading comprehension. However, while taking note of the warning that cloze procedure may operate differently in some subject areas, we must not lose sight of the two great advantages which cloze testing has in readability work. First, it allows us to gain data on the comprehensibility of passages without the need for the time-consuming item construction which would otherwise be necessary. Secondly, it does not simply predict the difficulty which a group might have with a text; it measures that difficulty directly. In doing so it is sensitive to individual differences and previous knowledge in a way which a predictive formula cannot be.

Carroll's second question relates to the possibility that a cloze test may be a different kind of test for different types of reader. Is a cloze readability test a different instrument when taken by good rather than poor readers? The work of Neville and Pugh appears to suggest that it is, but what is not so clear is what effect such a difference would have on the classroom use of cloze procedure as a readability measure; further research is necessary to provide an answer.

The third question, on the practical utility of cloze in the classroom, relates to the reliability of cloze test results. In large-scale research cloze results are more reliable because any individual variations are balanced out through randomisation. In general, it seems that results based on groups of less than about 30 may be unreliable. Certainly it would be inappropriate to assume that individual scores on cloze tests are as reliable as pooled results. Similarly, reliability can be improved by increasing the number of items included in a cloze test, or the number of samples taken from a book. There is some evidence to suggest that taking a number of samples is not always necessary; what is more important is that the passages are of reasonable length, and contain between 35 and 50 deletions.

The issue of what percentage of correct answers represents an adequate level of comprehension is clearly one on which more work needs to be done. Classroom teachers can use the experimental evidence reported in this chapter as an initial basis for interpreting cloze scores, but until more research findings are available, they must supplement the evidence with observation and deduction. Once cloze scores have been obtained for a group whose reading preferences and attainments are known, further cloze tests can be set against earlier results and a more specific interpretation of percentage scores can be developed. Small changes in the composition of a group should not invalidate these results, and this type of small-scale research could serve a number of purposes. The individual scores could be used as an index of progress; in addition to measuring the readability of texts in use in the classroom, the group's scores can be used to help evaluate courses and contribute to the inservice work of a department in a school.

It would be unfortunate if cloze procedure and readability formulae were regarded as mutually exclusive approaches to readability work. They are very different types of measure, and both are worthy of serious consideration. Cloze procedure can be particularly valuable when the group or the text under consideration is atypical, as it is better equipped to take account of local conditions. However, it takes more time to obtain cloze scores than it does to compute a formula score, and the teacher should be concerned therefore to ensure that the tests are carefully constructed and administered, and that the results are used to the benefit of the children who co-operated by completing the cloze tests.

5   Guidelines for applying readability measures in the classroom

In this chapter we first stress the need for caution in choosing and interpreting a readability score. We then consider guidelines for selecting and using readability measures with different age levels and subjects: infant and junior; middle and upper junior; secondary – English, mathematics, science and social studies; functional literacy materials.

Pitfalls and dangers

In this chapter we shall examine what appear to be the most appropriate and effective means of using readability measures with different age-groups and in different subject areas. We argued in Chapter 3 that with the exception of the Fry graph (which in any case is not a formula), there is no readability measure which is suitable for all age levels. It is worth while, therefore, to assess which formulae appear to be most useful at different age levels, and also to consider any special problems or pitfalls which may attend the use of formulae in different curricular areas.

Those who wish to refer directly to the readability measures recommended for materials for different age levels can refer to Figure 5.1 (p. 115). But remember the following:

- A readability score is only useful if the measure is a valid one and if the prose is suitable for analysis.
- A reading level score is only accurate if the formula is a reliable one and the counts of linguistic features have been made accurately on an adequate text sample.
- A readability score gives only an approximate indication of difficulty, accurate to about plus-or-minus one year or US grade.

- Generally speaking, it is reasonable to assume that children can cope with texts up to two years above their own reading level provided that *either* the teacher's close support is available, *or* the child's motivation is high.
- Never use a formula score to deny children access to what they *want* to read, but rather use a high score as a warning of potential difficulties ahead and the need for increased vigilance.

Infant and lower junior levels

As George Maginnis has pointed out (Maginnis, 1969), one of the problems in applying a formula to infant or beginning reader material is that the text samples are often too short to provide even a single 100-word sample. If a formula is based on variables such as *number of syllables per 100 words* or *number of full-stops per 100 words* it is necessary to calculate the number of syllables or sentences which would be present if the passage were longer (assuming that difficulty level remained constant). This can be done quite simply. Suppose a book was 84 words long, contained 16 sentences, and had 92 syllables. The general form of the sum we need to work out is:

Number of syllables or sentences per 100 words =

$$\frac{\text{Actual number of syllables or sentences} \times 100}{\text{Total number of words}}$$

Thus, to calculate the number of sentences per 100 words we put 16 as the actual number, and obtain:

$$\frac{16 \times 100}{84} = 19.0 \text{ sentences per 100 words}$$

Similarly, we put 92 as the actual number and find that the number of syllables per 100 words is:

$$\frac{92 \times 100}{84} = 109.6 \text{ syllables per 100 words}$$

Making this kind of arithmetic transformation does not invalidate a formula score. In fact, most computer programs work in a similar way and calculate a score on the basis of the full passage input, whether it is 84 or 20,000 words long. There is also no problem of sampling adequacy, in that if the whole of a book is analysed, there is no possibility of obtaining an inaccurate score from a partial analysis. It should be noted, however, that 50 words is generally taken to be a length below which samples might not be able to qualify as suitable for analysis. Readability formulae were not constructed in order to be applied at the single sentence level, and it would be inappropriate to use them in such a way. The FORCAST formula does not include a sentence length variable, and thus depends solely on the vocabulary used, but Sticht and his collaborators stipulated a 150-word sample as the normal one for analysis, so clearly they were wanting samples to be based on a reasonably long passage.

One problem of validity which occurs in considering the readability of primers is that of the normality of the vocabulary and syntactic structures. Formulae were derived from an analysis of the linguistic features of narrative or expository prose written by authors whose aim was to communicate and inform, not to teach how to read. To this extent it would appear invalid to apply a formula to prose which does not approximate in vocabulary or syntax to normal prose. As Huey noted in 1908:

Next to the beauty of the primers, the most striking thing about at least three-fourths of them is the inanity and disjointedness of their reading content, especially in their earlier parts. No trouble has been taken to write what a child would naturally say about the subject in hand, nor indeed, usually, to say *anything* connectedly or continuously, as even an adult would talk about the subject. (Huey, 1968, p. 279)

Perhaps the proportion of reading primers with inane and disjointed prose is now less than three-quarters, but most primary teachers will be acquainted with more than one scheme which uses what has been called 'fractured English'. Such schemes may or may not have their place in terms of teaching children how to read, but it is, strictly speaking, invalid to apply a readability formula to them, and any use of a formula on such material should take account of this danger.

In considering which measures to use with infant or lower junior material, it must be noted that many formulae have a 'floor effect', i.e. they do not produce reading age levels which are low enough to be of any value to primary teachers. The lowest Flesch score which can be obtained is ten years, and the lowest SMOG age level is eight years, so these formulae are out of the reckoning, at least in infant schools. The Fry graph, especially the versions which show an extension through to pre-primer level, has been found to be useful in infant schools, and there is no reason why it should not continue to be valuable.

The two formulae which seem most suitable for application at infant and lower junior level are the Spache formula and the Powers, Sumner and Kearl recalculation of the Flesch formula. Both these measures have a good research pedigree, and they differentiate usefully between texts from a reading level of six upwards. Of the two, the Spache formula is to be preferred, provided the teacher can find time to do the extra work needed to check whether words are included among the Dale list of 769 words (which is printed in Appendix B of this book). If time is short, the Powers–Sumner–Kearl formula should be used. In simple texts, counting syllables is relatively rapid, especially if one uses the shortcut of assuming that every word has one syllable and just counts the 'extra' syllables.

Finally, we must take account of the point made by Cliff Moon and Bridie Raban (1975, p. 77) in their book *A Question of Reading*. This is that at beginning reader level, the factors of length of a book and interrelationship of text and illustrations may be more crucial than at any other time in a child's reading life. If a readability measure is used, therefore, its score should only be considered as one factor among many contributing to reading difficulty.

Middle and upper junior levels

The middle junior age-range (i.e. seven to ten years of age) is undoubtedly the one on which most readability work has been focussed, and quite rightly, since it is during the years when a child is beginning to gain independence in reading that the task of matching a reader to a text is at its most delicate. A child whose fluency is only just beginning to develop may well have his or her confidence badly shaken by consecutive experiences of failure with a self-chosen book or a workbook. Furthermore, at this stage children are only beginning to acquire the compe-tence to monitor consciously their own reading performance, and, unless care is taken to prevent it, they may continue reading a book which is beyond them and reinforce errors while also developing an inappropriate notion of what constitutes a satisfactory level of comprehension.

So many specialists have already done valuable spadework in the area of assessing middle junior materials that it would be shortsighted and inefficient to fail to take account of their work. Readability analyses, whether based on formulae or on summative evaluations of classroom effectiveness (or both) take time and effort to produce, and we should always attempt to establish whether some other teacher or group has scored and evaluated the books or resources before us. University education department libraries and many colleges contain dissertations and theses on reading by the dozen, and local teachers' groups really should consider gaining access to them if it can be arranged; such an effort could save a great deal of wasted labour.

Certain regional and national groups in the United Kingdom have been particularly active in their field, and three widely known sources are listed below.

Centre for the Teaching of Reading at Reading University. This centre produces valuable classroom-based evaluations of reading materials, many of which have readability levels included. The centre also publishes two highly regarded monographs in which there are numerous reports on the difficulty level of schemes and courses based on *baseline gradings*, i.e. what children could actually cope with. These are Cliff Moon's *Individualised Reading* and Bridie Raban's *Reading Skill Acquisition*. Information can be obtained from Betty Root, the tutor in charge of the centre, which is based at the University of Reading, Berkshire.

National Association for Remedial Education. Many teachers will have used the wide-ranging lists of gradings compiled by Atkinson and Gains (1973). The gradings are determined by a mixture of classroom trials and readability analysis, and the books listed are not ones whose use is confined to slow or failing readers. The original list has been revised, and no doubt further revisions will continue to ensure the value of this book.

United Kingdom Reading Association. The UKRA produces an annual monograph *Books in School,* which gives brief reviews and readability scores on a large range of books and reading resources. Initially the readability scores were based on the FOG formula, with the inevitable result that texts were given scores which tended to be unreliably high. More recently, the measure used has been the Fry graph, which is less flamboyant at the top end of the difficulty range, and yet can also cope with primary material down to infant level.

When choosing a formula for use at middle or upper junior level, we need to consider whether it will yield reasonably reliable age levels. The problem of a 'floor effect' is less acute than at infant level; nevertheless because of their validity and reliability we shall recommend the use of the two form-ulae – those of Spache, and Powers, Sumner and Kearl – which were suggested for infant and lower junior level, and also one other measure, the Mugford formula and chart.

Overall, the Spache formula is generally considered to be the best for middle and upper junior school analyses, and it is the one used in a computerised form by the reading centre at Reading University. It produces a good spread of reading level scores, and the vocabulary variable (percentage of words on the Dale 769 list) is a sensitive one. The reason Spache's formula is not so effective with materials above a reading level of about thirteen years is that the proportion of words on the list begins to become constant with more difficult material; the Dale–Chall formula (which uses the 3,000-word list) is then necessary for meaningful discrimination.

A reading level of approximately ten years turns out to be a slightly difficult one to accommodate. With the exceptions of the Fry graph, Spache formula and Mugford formula, the other measures we introduced in Chapter 3 are at one end or other of their normal range, and are therefore a little suspect. In making a readability analysis therefore, one should hazard a guess about the probable level which seems to be indicated by skimming the text, and then choose the appropriate formula. This is not as random as it might appear: most teachers will be able to opt for a measure which will be appropriate for their needs most of the time, and it should not be necessary to find oneself in the position of needing to use a number of formulae. In order to simplify the choice, Figure 5.1 gives the range over which the measures recommended in this chapter are most reliable, and from this it is clear that two formulae at most will suffice to meet the average teacher's needs.

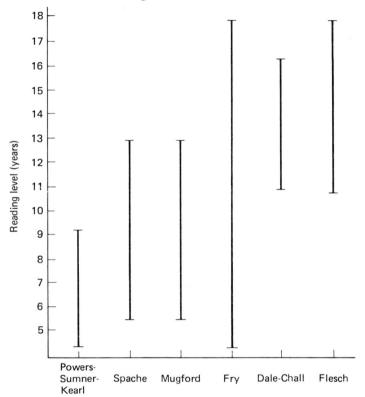

Figure 5.1. Range over which six recommended readability measures are most reliable in predicting reading level

When is it most important to gather and utilise readability data in the junior school? We have already suggested that it is during the years immediately after a child leaves the security and predictability of a reading scheme that close attention needs to be given to monitoring the material which is read, and this means non-fiction as well as fiction. In one survey, Leonard Hill

(1978) reported that in a stratified random selection which analysed 240 junior school library books, non-fiction material was found to be much more difficult than fiction. Using the Fry graph, Hill found that while the relatively small stocks of books for seven- and eight-year-olds were suitable in terms of prose difficulty for the intended age-groups, further up the school there was a great deal of material which was far beyond the reading attainment of any child in the school concerned. Furthermore, the school was one which if anything had given rather more attention to the selection of books than is usual in junior schools. Hill also reported that at the crucial level of nine to ten years, appropriate fiction was in short supply, and appropriate factual material scarcer still. These findings confirm many of the reports which were collected by the Schools Council Effective Use of Reading project team on their visits to English education authorities during 1973–76.

To sum up therefore, at middle and upper junior levels, readability measurement is most important for the materials of children who are just beginning to acquire the fluency to read and choose books independently. The second priority is to monitor the materials of children whose motivation to read is low, and who would regress or develop a negative attitude towards reading if they met with texts which reinforced the sense of failure (and this will include poor or failing readers of any age). The third priority is to be aware of the potential difficulty of information books, not simply because they are usually the most difficult books in the school, but also because they are often used in independent study for project or topic work, when the teacher's assistance is not readily available.

Secondary-school level

Figure 5.1 gives an indication of the age level accuracy of the readability measures which it is suggested are most reliable for secondary-school use, (i.e. age eleven to eighteen). The figure draws upon a number of research findings, but at secondary level in particular, use has been made of the findings of a survey carried out by the Effective Use of Reading project in Nottinghamshire during 1975 (Lunzer and Gardner, 1979). Texts used at first-year and fourth-year level (i.e. with groups aged eleven to twelve and fourteen to fifteen) in one school district over one week were collected, and altogether 125 texts from the subject areas of English, mathematics, science and social studies were analysed by computer, using a version of the program listed in Appendix C in this volume. The specific results will be referred to later, but the point here is that this exercise allowed one to examine how various formulae behaved when applied to a wide variety of material, which ranged from young children's fiction to science textbooks, and from poetry to worksheets. Teachers were also asked to rate the difficulty level of the passages, and this allowed the team to assess the age level accuracy of the formulae used. The relevant conclusions are summarised below.

- The Dale–Chall formula was best overall, although it is time-consuming to calculate.
- The Flesch formula was also a valid and generally reliable index of difficulty, and useful since it is widely known and relatively straightforward to calculate.
- The Fry graph, though not strictly a formula, also produced valid and reliable results.
- Mugford's formula and chart was high on validity at lower secondary level (though less reliable above a reading level of thirteen), and it appeared to be particularly valuable for assessing material for slower or failing readers.
- Two formulae, the SMOG and FOG indices, produced scores on most material which were higher than pooled teachers' estimates, and on difficult material gave very high scores (i.e. reading levels of above twenty years) which were difficult to interpret.

Readability measures are statistical tools, and it is up to the teacher to decide whether it is appropriate to apply them to a text. Generally speaking, it is only valid to use a formula on narrative or expository prose, and any deviation from this can be dangerous. Worksheets present an obvious problem: many worksheets are a mixture of headings, brief instructions and more continuous prose, and yet many teachers would want to evaluate them using a formula. This can only be done if (a) the analysis is confined to continuous prose, and (b) there is an absolute minimum of 50 words for analysis, and preferably 100 or more. If such a text sample is not available, then it might be worth considering giving the children a cloze test, but again the results might be unreliable if there were not enough items to form a stable test.

One issue which troubles many teachers at secondary level is whether it is reasonable to apply a readability formula to texts with a highly specific linguistic register. A modern textbook for seventeen-year-olds, for example, often covers ground which a decade ago was only studied at university or college level, and the vocabulary and style sometimes appear so esoteric that it seems nonsensical to consider their readability for the average reader. Consider the following passages:

The reactions with hydroxylamine, phenylhydrazine and 2.4-dinitrophenylhydrazine are used for the characterisation of aldehydes and ketones because the products are mostly crystalline solids and the melting points of the derivatives from closely similar aldehydes or ketones are usually sufficiently different to enable the carbonyl compound to be recognised.

The short track across the warmer waters of the North Sea from Holland to Norfolk had resulted in warming at the surface to give an almost D.A.L.R. in the cP air below 940 mbar. Above the inversion was warmer maritime air from the Atlantic with still warmer mT air above the near isothermal layer from 700 mbar to 650 mbar.

If in the binomial distribution we put $p = 0.1$ and $n = 5$, then the mean $np = 0.5$. In Table 10.2 the frequencies for the binomial distribution $10000(0.9 + 0.1)^5$ are given, and it is interesting to compare them with the Poisson frequencies above. In Table 11.1 the binomial frequencies for a constant value of $p = 0.1$ and different values of n are compared with the Poisson frequencies of distributions with the same means. It is obvious that as n increases and p decreases the agreement between the frequencies improves.

In each of these the vocabulary is dense and the extracts are virtually incomprehensible to a non-specialist. Each of these books has 100-word sections which place them firmly at the college level on the Fry graph, which means a reading level of over seventeen years, but one would not wish to assert that difficulties for the reader were caused by prolix style or unnecessarily complex vocabulary. It is rather that the specificity of the language is such that it is incomprehensible without an adequate background knowledge of the subject. To put it another way, a teacher might wrongly assume that a certain text was difficult to comprehend because an author was failing to control readability factors, when in fact it could be the semantic and conceptual complexity inherent in the subject which were leading to incomprehension.

The importance of readability varies according to the nature of the reader. This crucial fact, which has been substantiated by two careful research studies (reported in Klare, 1976), means for example that when the reader's knowledge of a subject is high to begin with, the effect of producing a more readable version is negligible. In the top years of secondary schools we are often dealing with such high-knowledge groups. When rewritten materials are used with low-knowledge groups, however, differences in comprehension favouring the more readable versions are much more likely to be found. In the eleven to sixteen age-range, therefore, when children are still studying a wide variety of subjects, readability is more important. However, it may become more important with higher age-groups if the efforts to encourage more students to continue their full-time education beyond the age of sixteen are successful.

One final point: when using a formula, you should not be tempted to alter it in any way. If a formula's results seem to be consistently one year too high or too low on a known set of materials, it is natural to make a mental note of the fact for future reference. What would invalidate the use of the formula however, would be to change arbitrarily the weighting of one of the variables in order to get the formula to produce the desired scores. Similarly, the use of Dale–Chall or Spache formulae is invalid if the tester deviates from the lists as published. To do so is comparable to buying spare parts for a car from a back-street garage: the car may appear to function well, but the guarantee which the manufacturer offered no longer applies.

Readability in specific subject areas

English

If they have heard of them at all, most secondary-school English teachers have a deep-rooted mistrust of readability formulae. This is as it should be. If members of the English department do not ensure that colleagues use formulae with circumspection, there is always a danger that they may be applied indiscriminately and harmfully. But readability measures can serve a useful, though limited role in the English classroom.

The most valuable role a formula can play is in assisting a teacher to choose the most appropriate novels or stories for individual children. There are now over 1,000 titles in the Puffin paperback series alone, and if we add to this number the books in the excellent Heinemann Windmill series we find approaching 1,500 titles. A teacher new to the profession, or one who changes schools, may well encounter year-group reading lists on which only a small fraction of the books are familiar. Equally, in the difficult area of books for less fluent readers, or for 'reluctant readers', teachers now have a bewildering variety of choice. As teachers become more familiar with the field of children's literature they no doubt gain in skill in interpreting publishers' blurbs and in being able to make a general assessment of a book. Nevertheless, the point made at the outset still stands – namely that in the specific task of assessing the difficulty of prose we are, as individuals, rather unreliable. As at junior level, it is with the poorer readers that most care needs to be taken, because it is such readers whose motivation is most likely to be damaged by the experience of failure to cope with a book. Even so, readability data should be used as a warning of potential difficulties, and not as the exclusive basis for matching a child to a novel. The child's own interests, and the kind of material he or she has read previously will be at least as important as the prose difficulty level in helping to decide what to choose.

The readability measures which seem most appropriate for secondary use on the basis of the Effective Use of Reading project's research are those of Dale–Chall, Flesch, Mugford and Fry. Each of these is reasonably reliable in terms of age level, but for novels it would probably suffice to use the rank-ordering of difficulty which readability scores can provide. Initially, rank-ordered results will be of limited value; it is only when a teacher knows some of the books well that rankings will acquire a significance. After a while, however, rank-ordered results can be more informative than age levels, because while an age level is a number in isolation, the rank-ordering relates the newly analysed book to the others on one's list, and the teacher can see which books are at about the same level, and which ones might be a little more approachable. Often in subjects such as science or history, there are fewer possibilities for direct comparisons between textbooks, and in such a case, a teacher may have to depend on the reading level alone.

We have stressed before that text samples for readability analysis must be composed of expository or narrative prose, because otherwise to use a formula is invalid. The James Joyce and Gertrude Stein examples from Chapter 3 made this clear, but this puts an onus on the teacher to decide *in advance* whether or not a sample is suitable for analysis. Generally, therefore, one would not expect to analyse poetry, or prose which is essentially poetic, because the results would need extremely careful interpretation.

One researcher who did use a formula on samples of poetry was J. A. Allard. In a study undertaken in the 1940s (cited in Klare, 1963, p. 222), Allard examined what factors in poetry tended to be associated with children's preferences. Following the penchant for large-scale surveys of readability which were popular twenty years before, Allard examined the preferences of 50,000 children, and presented them with 673 poems. His main conclusion was that vocabulary difficulty in particular was associated with a child's disliking a poem. It would also be interesting to know whether this implies that complex syntax was less important as a factor than we might intuitively feel when choosing poems for children, and that provided they can cope with the vocabulary, children will not tend to dislike poems because they used unfamiliar syntactic structures. Klare's citation does not provide enough information to resolve this, but the conclusion is compatible with Allard's results, and it might be worthy of further investigation.

In the Effective Use of Reading project's survey, it was found that within the books and worksheets in use in the schools visited, there was a mean reading level of 12.4 years in first-year secondary classes, where the mean age of the children is 12.0 years at the mid-point of the school year. As Table 5.1 demonstrates, this was only half a year below the mean reading level of English material three years further up the school. This finding has prompted some teachers to ask whether we are making sufficient demands of students at the age of fifteen, but another interpretation is possible. As we have already noted, readability

Table 5.1. Readability survey results at first-year and fourth-year secondary-school levels

	First year			Fourth year		
	Number of passages	Reading level (years)	Standard deviation	Number of passages	Reading level (years)	Standard deviation
English	17	12.4	1.2	23	12.9	1.4
Mathematics	5	11.3	0.6	15	12.7	1.7
Science	9	13.5	2.3	12	14.0	1.8
Social studies	22	13.0	2.3	22	14.1	2.2
Average	53	12.73		72	13.60	

Results derived from Flesch formula grade scores
From the schools council Effective use of Reading project (Lunzer and Gardner, 1979)

matters more when motivation is low, and English teachers are painfully aware that between the ages of thirteen and sixteen many children's motivation to read drops depressingly low. The comparatively low average reading level at age fifteen could thus be an indication of the response of teachers to the need to offer poorly motivated readers easier prose, and an inspection of the books surveyed does support such a view. At first-year level (age eleven to twelve) such authors as Alan Garner and Leon Garfield are represented, while at fourth-year level, although there were some difficult books, novels such as *Billy Liar* and *To Sir, With Love* kept the average reading level down. In parenthesis we should note that although some passages which were clearly poetic were analysed (these were from *Macbeth*, *Journey of the Magi* and *Under Milk Wood*), this was done solely for completeness. The results were not biassed as a result, because oddly enough the works all produced scores close to the average for the fourth-year of 12.9 years.

As long ago as 1937, readability formulae were attacked as not being able to assess the literary value of a book. They still cannot, and neither can they assess a child's interests and emotional needs. For English teachers, therefore, readability formulae must have a subordinate role, but it can be a useful one, especially if teachers take the trouble to share results and exchange information on the widest practicable basis.

Mathematics

Since the introduction of many new concept-oriented courses in mathematics, there has been a good deal of debate about whether an undue emphasis has come to be placed on verbal learning, and mathematics textbooks have been subjected to very close scrutiny. The Effective Use of Reading team found that many mathematics teachers reported reading problems in their subject, not least at fourth- and fifth-form levels, as children approach public examinations. Interestingly enough, the picture which emerged from the readability survey results showed that the texts in use in schools were not excessively difficult, but nevertheless this did not necessarily imply that all was well.

Table 5.1 shows mathematics texts to be on average the easiest of the four major subject areas, but further explanation is necessary. At first-year level, from the ten schools involved in the survey only five samples of analysable mathematical prose were collected. Clearly, if a worksheet contains no more than the occasional *Expand:* or *Solve for x:* it is impossible to apply any readability measure other than the FORCAST formula, which has no sentence-length variable, and even this really requires 150-word samples. In short, while it may well be that there are many difficult mathematics textbooks in print, it seems that teachers are not tending to use them in class. The survey revealed that some schools were relying on their own worksheets while others were using books with traditional sets of exercises, but in either case there was practically no emphasis on expository prose. In the lessons the central focus was on operations rather than concepts, and the prose generally consisted of instructions to do a task rather than explanation or comment.

The emphasis in the survey texts on tasks rather than concepts helps to explain why the readability levels were low. As D. A. Johnson found in 1957 (cited in Klare, 1963, p. 233), what was called 'problem material', which presumably includes instructions for tasks and exercises, was found to be easier than 'expository or enrichment material'. It could be, therefore, that the reading survey mathematics results were artificially depres-

sed by this non-expository prose, and while the prose encountered by children in mathematics lessons is not complex, this
could indicate a possible source of difficulty later on. After all, in
English lessons the readable books used at fourth-year level are
a part of the fifth-year examination syllabuses. In mathematics,
by contrast, there is general agreement that there is a heavy
verbal component in the courses leading to the public
examinations. It may therefore be too much to expect children
suddenly to be able to cope with difficult material when they
have not been prepared for the challenge in previous years.

A further reason for examining readability scores on
mathematics material very closely is the compression and exac-
titude of the prose. The construct which forms the basis for most
readability formulae is a comprehension figure of 50% on the
McCall–Crabbs test passages, and this is clearly some distance
from total comprehension. In some subjects, skipping a word
here or misreading a word there will not have a damaging effect
on overall comprehension, but in mathematics it may alter the
meaning drastically. By training, mathematicians are
encouraged to prefer elegance and conciseness, but this in turn
may lead them to write textbook prose which contains less
redundancy than is present in other subject areas. This conciseness, and the corresponding need for close and accurate
reading, should lead us to view readability scores in
mathematics as potentially below the 'true' difficulty level of the
materials. Two formulae which have been designed specifically
for use with mathematics texts are known in the United States
(Kane, Hater and Byrne, 1974), but I am not aware of their
having been applied in the United Kingdom.

Finally, poor motivation is a problem in mathematics of which
teachers are always conscious. The Effective Use of Reading
project found that boys and girls concurred in rating the
mathematics samples as the most boring of the forty passages in
the study. This is not surprising, because allied to the
stereotyped view (which many children unfortunately acquire)
that the subject as a whole is boring is the fact that nearly all the
text samples were problems or tasks to be completed. There was
no trace of human interest or fun. This surely argues for a
greater use of the fascinating material from the wider world of
mathematics. Child prodigies, lost theorems, duels to the death,

artificial intelligence, chess, astronomy and computing are only a few of the possibilities which some teachers already use.

In an interesting American experiment Russell Call and Neal Wiggin (1974), a high-school head of mathematics and an English specialist, report what happened when the English specialist took over a mathematics class to teach a two-week unit on linear equations. Without any prior knowledge of algebra, even at the level at which he was about to teach it, the English teacher took the children through the unit, emphasising the concepts of linearity and dependence, and stressing wherever possible the meanings of key words and the relationships between ideas. After two weeks the class and a control group taught by the head of mathematics were tested. The results (which were carefully controlled for regression effects) showed a clear advantage to the group taught by the English teacher. The authors concluded that a developmental reading programme which included specialist subject areas was necessary for all children, because even fluent readers had difficulty with the reading in some subjects. This must imply a broadening of the reading curriculum in mathematics beyond tasks and instructions, and into areas which will allow for a range of purposes, responses and interests. This approach would be likely to increase motivation as well as deepen mathematical understanding.

Science

There is no curricular area in which materials have received more scrutiny from readability formulae as that of science. This may be because scientists are conscious of the reading difficulties apparent in many areas of their discipline. It could also be related to their preference for objective measurement. While literature specialists agonise over the danger of violating a book by applying a formula to it, science colleagues have analysed the readability of science books at every level from elementary school to college. Klare (1963), in his annotated bibliography, summarises over twenty research studies which were reported before 1960, and the results are fairly uniform. Science texts are castigated as 'too dull', 'too difficult', and too unstable in their difficulty level from one section of the book to another.

Studies by Rader and by Powers in the mid-1920s set the tone: science books had an unwarranted level of vocabulary difficulty, and biology was the biggest culprit of all. More recently William Graham (1978), writing in the *School Science Review*, has echoed this claim, and it was supported in the Effective Use of Reading project's research. The project team found that the science materials collected at first-year secondary level (i.e. for children aged 11.5–12.5) had a mean reading level of 13.5 years, which made science the most difficult subject analysed.

As in mathematics, the team found that books were in short supply at lower secondary level, and indeed the first-year samples were predominantly teacher-produced worksheets – if children did not have these they probably had no printed materials at all. There are two crucial points here. First, contrary to what one might predict, classroom teachers are just as taxing as published authors in terms of the difficulty level of the prose they write. Secondly, it appears likely that some of the problems encountered further up the school may be associated with the fact that children have had little previous contact with print, and have therefore had little opportunity to develop gradually a familiarity with scientific prose.

Science teachers are often conscious that even if they have a textbook for the class, it is difficult to find time to discuss the book's presentation of a topic because of the need to do practical work, demonstrations, blackboard work and tidying up before the bell goes and the laboratory is cleared. The result of this is that using the textbook becomes an aspect of homework, and this in turn creates extra problems for the students. It is common in the United States to assert that for independent study a book should be two years *easier* than the material used in class when the teacher is available to support and explicate. The Schools Council project research, however, found that the high level of text difficulty and tendency of teachers to set reading homework in science led to a slight positive correlation between difficulty of a text and its use in an unsupported context. In other words, the more difficult a book was, the more likely it would be that a reader would have been given it to work on for homework, without the teacher's help being available.

Some teachers who were interviewed by the project team reported that children had great difficulty in coping with science texts, and that as a result of this the teacher placed less emphasis on independent learning. This is not an easy trend to reverse:

children like what they do well at, and if they fail to cope with a book their motivation will quickly drop. If science teachers wish to encourage a greater use of printed sources in science, it does appear that they must consider using rather more approachable texts. It is not enough to protest that the text in question is only intended to be used as a reference point to support the teacher's efforts: ultimately what determines its usefulness is the extent to which it can contribute to independent learning.

Another aspect of applying a formula to scientific prose which worries some teachers is the repetition of certain key concepts. In an extended passage on *equilibrium*, runs the argument, each repetition of the word is associated with a greater possibility of comprehension, since the essential aim of the passage is to make the concept clear. Therefore it is inappropriate to count each occurrence of the word as five syllables; this will simply give a nonsensically high readability score. The flaw in this argument is that we cannot assume that successive repetitions of the word *are* easier to comprehend. They might be, if the explanations are clear, but there is no necessary connection, and one could argue that some readers would become increasingly mystified and frustrated if comprehension did not come quickly. It is therefore perfectly proper to score each occurrence of every word, and indeed it might be invalid not to do so.

A similar refutation can be offered to the argument that figures and illustrations have the express purpose of clarifying the text, and, since they are an integral part of the communication the author is wishing to make, they can lower its readability level. We did admit the possible value of illustrations in the case of infant level books, but it must be stressed that illustrations do not of themselves make the reading level of the prose any lower. They mediate between the prose and the reader, but that is not the same as lowering its difficulty level, and an author cannot claim immunity to the charge of writing incomprehensible prose simply because the prose is accompanied by good diagrams. A reader needs to read the test in order to find his way to the diagrams, and if it is incomprehensible he may never reach them.

In applying readability measures to scientific prose the most likely problem is that of having a passage which jumps disconcertingly from verbal into symbolic language, as the following sentence demonstrates.

The apparatus used is shown in Figure 1, the flask being charged with 50 cm^3 of 2-volume hydrogen peroxide solution and 5 cm^3 of 2 M alkali.

This passage is on the limit of what may be meaningfully subjected to readability analysis. If there were any more symbols it would have to be viewed as too remote from normal prose, and in such a case a teacher would have to use cloze tests or some other form of classroom trial to obtain some information about children's reactions. Some writers on readability would recommend articulating and then counting syllables on the basis of the spoken version, but this is not always reliable. Edward Fry (1977) has stated a preference for scoring each symbol as one syllable, so *1978* would count as four and *pH* as two. In order to ensure validity, it is recommended that Fry's graph is computed as he wishes it to be, but for other purposes the rules given in Chapter 3 still stand: a word is defined as a string of alphanumeric characters delimited by spaces or punctuation marks, and for consistency the number of syllables allocated to a word in the absence of any printed vowels is one. Thus, *1978, pH, WVS* and *Cu(NH$_3$)$_2$* should all be scored as single-syllable words. If such a procedure appears likely to have a significant affect on the readability score, then the use of a formula is probably invalid, and another method of assessing difficulty should be used.

Social studies

The use of this general term to encompass history, geography, sociology and religious education is necessary both because of its ubiquity in American research and because in English schools such a wide variety of courses are currently run in these areas that without such a term comparison of approaches is not possible. Naturally one acknowledges that as in science, not all subjects are equal in terms of areas of difficulty, and geology in particular is an area in many integrated humanities courses which appears to have the most difficult vocabulary.

Writing in the 1930s about the reading difficulties in social studies, Horn (cited in Chall, 1958, pp. 126–7) cautioned against the uncritical use of readability measures in this subject area,

and he listed nine factors which he felt were important con-
tributors to difficulties in social studies. These were as follows:

(1) Conceptual complexity
(2) Poor style
(3) Structural complexity (including vocabulary and syntax)
(4) Precision with which words are used
(5) The need to understand word meanings in context
(6) Heavy burden of new vocabulary
(7) The need to take account of students' individual differences
(8) The poorer student's need for additional factual detail and illustration
(9) Factors to which a formula is insensitive: conceptual difficulty,
meagreness of treatment, inaccuracies, etc.

In support of his sixth point, on vocabulary load, Horn quoted
the conclusions of the psychologist E. L. Thorndike, which were
that new words and technical terms should not appear at too
short intervals. Specifically, Thorndike's suggestion was that
new words should not be introduced more often than one per
200 words. One must admit that this seems a stringent demand
to place on a textbook author, and it is not surprising that Horn
found that many books did not fulfil his criterion.

The Effective Use of Reading survey found (see Table 5.1) that
social studies texts were generally slightly above the reading
level of the children with whom they were used at first-year
secondary level. They were also on average the most difficult
texts of all at fourth-year level. An additional potential problem
was the great variety of materials in use. The standard deviation
of 2.3 years in Table 5.1 indicates that there was as great a
variety of levels in social studies materials as in any other subject
area, and while this could imply a responsiveness to the needs
of individual children, one must also remark that texts with a
reading level of above fifteen years are likely to be valuable for a
tiny minority of twelve-year-olds, and the basis for sampling
was to examine books which teachers were using with 'average'
groups in their schools.

Teachers of social studies vary from geographers with a
scientific and statistical training to historians, sociologists and
theologians who have a literary and artistic basis for their higher
education. Perhaps for this reason, there are occasionally disagreements within the discipline about the usefulness of objective measures of text difficulty. For example, a number of

teachers who made use of the Humanities Curriculum Project materials (Stenhouse, 1970, 1973) reported that they seemed too difficult for the fourteen- and fifteen-year-old early school leavers at which they were aimed. A study by Barbara Turner (1971) used cloze scores to evaluate students' ability to cope with the reading material of the project, and the results showed that most students obtained less than 40% correct answers (the lowest acceptable score compatible with comprehension) on most of the passages analysed. Furthermore, since one objective of the Humanities Curriculum Project is to encourage independent learning, with the teacher acting as a neutral chairman, it seems likely that students' reading comprehension of the materials may have been poorer than if more direct teaching support had been available. For Lawrence Stenhouse, however, the project's director, this research finding will not have caused distress. In the supporting material for the course, he explains that his explicit aim is to encourage young adults to test themselves against difficult books and extracts, and that his expectations of what children might gain from their reading are not unrealistic. If children can gain an insight into such concepts as justice or truth, for example, by consulting and discussing extracts from difficult books, including primary sources to which such less able students do not normally have access, then the materials will have served their purpose.

It is clear that in the social studies area, users of any objective measures of text difficulty will have to consider carefully the use to which materials are to be put, before deciding whether a particular book or passage is suitable for a group. This point, however, is one which applies to all subject areas, and it does not invalidate the use of formulae. It rather reminds us of the need for caution in interpreting the results.

The Schools Council's project Reading for Learning in the Secondary School has looked at some of the problems of compression in history texts. One factor associated with compression which we touch upon in Chapter 6 is the use made of anaphoric reference, i.e. reference back to other nouns or phrases, and the project team are analysing the difficulties for the reader which occur if anaphora is used too little, or inappropriately. Readability formula scores do give a general indication of passage difficulty in social studies, but the team are also applying the propositional analysis used by Kintsch (1974) to obtain an index of difficulty. Kintsch found that the number of propositions in a sentence was a better predictor of sentence recall than the simple number of words per sentence. Propositions are not easy to count, but broadly speaking they consist of a *relational term* and one or more *arguments*. Thus *George hit John* consists of the relational term *hit*, and the arguments *George* and *John*. The advantage of Kintsch's system is that it allows one to break down a sentence into its constituent propositions in such a way that the overall complexity can be described. We shall not elaborate the system here, but it showed, for example, that although the following sentences differ in length by only two words, the first is based on only four propositions, while the second is based on eight:

Romulus, the legendary founder of Rome, took the women of the Sabine by force. (Four propositions.)
Cleopatra's downfall lay in her foolish trust of the fickle political figures of the Roman world. (Eight propositions.)

This type of analysis is extremely time-consuming, and at present it remains essentially a research tool, but it offers an approach to quantifying idea density, which has proved one of the most elusive factors in readability work. Research into propositional structure along the lines Kintsch has proposed is relatively new, but it is important in two respects: first it is refining the hitherto amorphous concept of idea density, and secondly it is a mode of analysis which can take us beyond the word and sentence levels, and towards a description of the information structure of a whole passage. It seems likely that this will become an increasingly important factor of readability research.

Functional literacy

This book addresses itself primarily to schoolteachers, but before leaving the issue of applying measures of text difficulty in a practical context it is worth looking at some of the important work which has been done on functional literacy.

In the BBC's handbook for adult literacy tutors (Longley, 1975) there are many practical tips, and for readability measurement the use of the Fry graph is recommended. Fry's graph is easy to use, and it has the additional advantage in work where a wide range of potential difficulty is anticipated of being reasonably reliable over a wide range of age levels.

A readability formula which was developed especially for use with adult materials was that of Tom Sticht and his collaborators on the HumRRO project for the US Army. His formula, the FORCAST index, is given in Chapter 3. It is unusual in that it requires 150-word text samples (whereas most formulae require multiples of 100 words) and it includes no sentence-length variable. This formula was found on the Effective Use of Reading project to produce poorer correlations with pooled teacher judgments than other formulae which included a sentence-length variable. But the omission of such a variable can sometimes be an advantage: it enables a teacher to obtain an estimate of the difficulty level of texts in which normal sentence patterns are violated or indeed no full stops are printed, such as technical manuals or notices.

Sticht constructed his formula by analysing essential job reading materials, most of which were instructional or technical in content. The formula he produced was aimed for a young male adult population, and this factor needs to be taken into account when the formula is used in other contexts. The FORCAST formula was one of a number which his research produced, but the one finally chosen had the advantage of being simple and readily applicable by clerical personnel without any special training or equipment. In an extensive research project Sticht (1972) reported that one significant finding concerned the preference of poor readers for an oral presentation of information. The poorer readers, however, scored no more highly on tests of orally presented information compared with when they were given printed instructions, which might imply that the FORCAST formula measures 'listenability' as well as readability.

A further aspect of Sticht's research (Sticht, 1973) was an investigation of the reading grade levels required by army personnel in various jobs. This is an extremely important issue, but unfortunately it is one about which there has been a good deal more speculation than research. Sticht's findings were (changing the grade levels to age levels by adding 5) that for the cook's job a competence equal to that of the average reader in the age-range 11.0–11.9 years was required. For repairmen the range was 12.0–12.9 years, and for supply clerks the range was 12.0–14.9. Clearly these figures related solely to job-oriented reading, and did not take account of other areas of life in which reading is important.

There are a number of types of material in use in school which are difficult to analyse using a conventional formula. Forms, questionnaires, some instructional worksheets, labels and posters may all be unsuitable for analysis because presentation and lay-out conventions do not really allow one to estimate sentence length in the normal way. Multiple-choice tests and examination questions would also often come into this category. In such cases, and if it is not practicable to use a cloze test or to obtain subjective ratings, it would be reasonable to consider using the FORCAST formula in order to predict the text difficulty. It is important to note, however, that in the Effective Use of Reading project's validation study this formula was not as accurate a predictor of difficulty as other formulae, and it tended to give results on lower school materials which were rather high. Nevertheless, provided these facts are taken into account there is no reason why the FORCAST formula should not be used, particularly with technical materials.

6 The use of readability data in writing texts

In this chapter we consider some of the research evidence which can help us to produce more readable writing. Two warnings are given: first, it can be futile to write to some strict formula; secondly, the total curriculum context cannot be ignored. Children's own views can be usefully sought, but specific attention can also be given to vocabulary and syntax, and to making clear the organisation of the information which is to be presented.

The problem and the dangers

The greatest part of this book has been concerned with predicting or measuring the difficulty of texts. This emphasis reflects the fact that readability measures were constructed to be applied *post hoc* to texts already written. However, many teachers and reading specialists have naturally asked themselves whether it would be useful to apply such measures at the authorship stage, in order to produce at the outset reading material which would be more comprehensible to the intended audience. The line of argument taken in this chapter will be a pragmatic one: writing to a formula provides absolutely no guarantee that the resulting prose will be elegant or comprehensible; however, there are certain approaches and criteria which one can take into account which will increase the likelihood of a book or worksheet being more readable than would otherwise have been the case.

There is no inconsistency in saying that while it can be dangerous to write to a formula, writing more simply is indeed possible. The point is that readability formula scores tend to be determined by word length and sentence length, and if these are reduced the readability score will be lower, but this will not necessarily make the text more comprehensible. It tends to be the case that long words and long sentences are found in difficult prose, but it is not the word length and sentence length as such which are *causing* the difficulties; they are associated with it in a more complex and subtle way. If the relationship were simply a causal one, it would be easy enough to truncate every word down to its first syllable and to double the number of full-stops. This would soon lower the readability index, but whether anyone would be able to understand the resulting prose is another matter.

To a statistician this kind of application of research findings would be as unwarranted as responding to the knowledge that intelligence is positively correlated with height by stretching children on the rack. Nevertheless some teachers and educational publishers have come very close to assuming a causal relationship between formula variables and comprehensibility. In the 1950s, Edward Fry asserted that ill-advised use of formulae had produced dozens of unreadable textbooks in the United States. More recently, in England, the Avon Resources for Learning Development Unit (RLDU) discovered that using readability data at the authorship stage can cause problems.

The RLDU was established in the early 1970s to assist teachers in the Avon area by producing and distributing classroom materials in a number of different subjects. The unit aimed to help teachers who were working with mixed-ability groups by writing materials at up to five levels of difficulty. At an early stage, therefore, the team obtained a computer program which would help in the task of monitoring readability levels. Initially, when the readability scores were made available to the teachers and unit staff who were writing the new materials, the results were beneficial: the authors learned when it might be advisable to consider rewriting certain worksheets or sections of a booklet. After a time, however, the unit's directors began to realise that the readability results were becoming a much less reliable predictor of whether or not a worksheet needed to be rewritten. The reason for this was that the authors were writing prose which produced low readability scores, but not prose which poor readers could understand. Perhaps unconsciously, the authors had begun to manipulate word length and sentence length in order to lower the readability score, and the result was prose which at its worst was disjointed and incomprehensible.

As a result the team replanned their evaluation procedures, and placed less emphasis on readability formula results at the writing stage.

The decision of the RLDU's team to reconsider their use of readability data was entirely proper, and it does not invalidate the use of formulae in other situations. What it does do is to emphasise the point that rewriting, or writing more simply, is not a simple matter. The reason readability formulae results are valuable is because the two factors that most formulae measure are indeed associated with actual difficulty. It is the case that, in general, difficult ideas or concepts tend to be expressed in words which are comparatively infrequent, and such words tend to be longer than more common words. Similarly, complex ideas or lines of argument tend to be written in grammatically complex sentences. Consider this sentence:

If the assertion, that the understanding can employ its various principles and its various concepts solely in an empirical and never in a transcendental manner, is a proposition which can be known with certainty, it will yield important consequences.

This sentence from Kant's *Critique of Pure Reason* is not an easy one to understand unless the reader has studied philosophy and has some familiarity with Kant's work, and rewriting it is not at all easy. First of all the crucial terms *empirical* and *transcendental* are used in a very precise way, and would require a careful (and lengthy) gloss if they were to be avoided. Secondly, the logical form of the sentence is: 'If P (a proposition) can be known with certainty, it will yield important consequences'. The construction may seem to impose rather a heavy strain on short-term memory, but this too is difficult to avoid. Kant does not wish, at this point, to assert the proposition, and this makes it difficult to separate the proposition from the *if* clause associated with it. Indeed, to do so might actually make the sentence less comprehensible. The following sentence is a layman's attempt to simplify Kant's words:

If we can be sure that what we know can only be based on direct experience, and not on things in themselves, then this will have important consequences.

This rendering of Kant's sentence is an attempt to simplify it without losing the central thought of the original. Nevertheless it is still opaque, and it is more like a cartoon or caricature than a photograph or portrait of the original. It may be satisfactory or unsatisfactory, but either way it is thumbnail sketch of the argument, not a one-for-one mapping of the elements of the original. In particular, the use of the verb *know* in the simplified version would jar with a philosopher, because the employment of a concept is not the same as knowledge of it.

It is, therefore, naive to assume in advance that reading difficulty can be determined simply by manipulating sentence length and word length. Nevertheless, some highly reputable publishing firms have adopted just such an approach in briefing their authors. In a paper to the British Educational Research Association, the managing director of a firm which specialises in reading materials told his audience that his authors were given a highly specific remit for a graded series of reading materials. They were given a subject, such as *Snakes*, a specified number of words, of which a precise number had to be on the Dale list of 769 familiar words, and an exact number of sentences within which the passage was to be written. If the authors wrote a passage which was one word too long, or used one familiar word too many, it was emended by the editorial director. As a result, the materials were marketed as having two-month gradations of reading difficulty between passages.

This claim could be challenged on a number of grounds. The formula used was an *ad hoc* reworking of the Spache formula, with an altered word list and new variable weightings, and either of these changes would, strictly speaking, invalidate the use of the formula. More serious, though, was the claim to have produced passages which increased in reading difficulty by two-month stages. The most widely accepted formulae have a standard error of plus-or-minus about 0.85 of a year. In other words, a reading level of 10.5 years would suggest that the true difficulty probably lies somewhere in the range 9.65–11.35 years. We can also add that *probably* in this sense means *68% of the time*; i.e. in approximately one-third of cases the true difficulty is actually likely to be outside the seventeen-month range given here. Readability formula scores, as we have stressed repeatedly, are approximations, not micrometer measurements. The publisher's response to the challenge that his approach in no way guaranteed the validity of his claim was to quote from the teachers who had used his materials in pre-publication trials. These teachers had reported back if any passages were not comprehensible for the target group, or if they seemed much easier than was suggested by the readability score. These field trials, together with the considerable experience of his authors, helped to ensure that no inappropriate passages were included in the final published materials.

One is inclined to believe that these two extra perspectives on passage difficulty – authors' judgment and teachers' opinions from field trials – may have been by far the most important determinants of the accuracy of the final published reading levels. It could even be that this had been achieved in spite of, rather than because of, the strategy adopted by the publisher.

As was argued in the introduction to this book, the fact that readability measures are sometimes used in inappropriate ways is not an argument for prohibiting their use; what it does imply is the need for more information about when and how such measures should be used. The publishing firm referred to is highly reputable, and it is laudable that they should take the opportunity to promote an exchange of views with others in education about how best to prepare reading development materials. It is very easy for teachers to find themselves saying that educational publishers should take greater notice of teachers' opinions, children's interests, children's reading difficulties, and so on. For many years, and not only as a result of the Bullock report, most major educational publishers have been attempting to do precisely this. If progress has been slow, it has been for a number of good reasons: research costs money, and if schools do not have money to buy books, publishers can ill afford to invest in research; unlike researchers, publishers are in direct competition with each other, so it requires courage and foresight to begin to pool ideas and accelerate the process of sharing insights or information; publishers publish books, but they do not write them, and to this extent they cannot be held solely responsible for the prose style of their authors, most of whom are or have been teachers.

The importance of the curriculum

This book is not about the curriculum, but it is important to preface the sections on how to produce more readable materials with a reminder: producing effective material is only secondarily a matter of style – it is primarily a curricular issue. How and when is the material going to be used? By which teachers and with which groups? How are the reading materials going to be integrated into the rest of the department's work? How is individualised work going to relate to whole-class lessons, to practical work, and to exposition?

If a teacher or planning group has not begun to consider these and related questions, it would be inefficient to devote all its energies to attempting to write readable worksheets and to computing the readability levels of all the department's books.

Consider the following extract, which is from a worksheet formerly used with a mixed-ability group of fourteen-year-olds.

Describe a piece of shale which you can get from the front of the classroom. Write about it under the following headings:
(a) Colour.
(b) Thickness of the layers.
(c) Roughly how long would it have taken for enough mud to be deposited on the sea floor to form this specimen? (Sheet 1 will tell you the rate of formation.)
(d) How hard is it? Can it be scratched with a knife, a copper coin (softer) or with a finger nail (very soft)?
(e) What do the fine particles which have been scratched off feel like when rubbed between the fingers?
(f) Soak the specimen in water for a minute or two and then leave it to dry for another minute. Now put a drop of water on the rock and watch it carefully. Does the water soak into the rock?
(g) If the water soaks into the rock it is called POROUS rock. If the water does not it is called an IMPERMEABLE rock. Which is your specimen?
(h) In what way is the Shale different from the mud from which it was formed?

Why did some of the teachers in the school feel that the worksheet needed to be revised? They felt some children were not gaining very much from attempting the practical work. This in turn could have been because the passage was written in a style which was too difficult. However, although there is an occasional difficult word or phrase (such as *deposited, fine particles*, or *specimen*) the writing is generally quite simple. A readability analysis confirms this. The passage has a reading level on the Fry graph of about nine years, and the Flesch score (which we know tends to be a little high on easy materials) is eleven years. The school's head of resources had a coordinating role in the preparation of materials, and his feeling was that it was how the worksheets were being integrated into other work which was the crux of the matter.

The problem was that the crucial concepts on which the whole practical exercise was based, porosity and impermeability, were tacked on to the end of the work. The result of this was that the poor readers, who would probably work more slowly, might never reach those sections, and thus would inevitably have an imprecise idea of what they were doing and why they were doing it. In the event, many children became bored by what seemed to be aimless practical activities which were accompanied by rote learning of apparently arbitrary facts and technical terms.

What all the children needed, not least the slower learners, was a conceptual framework onto which the new learning could be mapped. Before beginning rewriting, therefore, the structure of the whole course was redesigned to allow every child, including the weaker pupils, an introduction to some key concepts at an early stage in each part of the course. The point here is that improving readability is only likely to be profitable if the course material itself is worthwhile. It would be dangerous to devote time to cosmetic surgery on a text while ignoring the possibility of an organic disease beneath its surface.

Using children's insights

Some poor readers are unreliable reporters of whether or not they are in difficulty with a text, but most of us know whether or not we are understanding what we read. This fact is one which we can turn to great advantage in considering rewriting classroom materials. In this section we shall look briefly at three ways of using children's own opinions of what is difficult in order to gain useful information.

One researcher has hit upon an extremely neat idea which seems likely to be used by both reading researchers and teachers in the future. He gave children copies of sections from textbooks and two pens, one red and one blue. What the children had to do was simply to underline in blue any sections which they thought were really easy, and to mark in red any they could not understand, or which seemed very difficult. The researcher then looked at each child's paper, and gave every word in the passage a score of 0, 1 or 2 according to whether it was marked in blue, ignored, or marked in red. The pooled scores thus provided a word-by-word analysis of the difficulty of the total passage. This method can easily be used in the classroom. For example, a class could be asked to underline difficult parts of a worksheet before going on to the next one. When they have all finished, the teacher would then have a permanent record of the group's problems, and it might give a valuable indication about which sections needed rewriting.

Children's opinions have also been used in some science classes in a way which could be useful in a number of subject areas. At the end of the academic year one teacher asked his pupils to write down all the words or phrases which had caused them difficulty during the previous year. The words were collated and put into booklets with a brief explanation, and the resulting glossaries were then hung up on the laboratory wall for the following year's classes to use for reference.

Every department in a school should have a clear idea about what concepts and technical terms are being used or introduced in each school year. This system of year-group glossaries for a subject at least allows this to be achieved retrospectively, and it also allows children the opportunity to alert the teacher to other words which might be causing problems. Ambiguous words such as *salt* or *solution* are notoriously difficult when a child's day might include lessons in domestic science, chemistry and mathematics, and the teachers may not be aware of the child's problems in accommodating to the different usages. If there was inter-departmental co-operation in preparing year-group glossaries teachers might have an opportunity to pinpoint such ambiguities, and to give children extra help in resolving them.

The third suggestion is much more controversial: the children could try to rewrite worksheets or particular sections of a book themselves. The discipline of having to understand and then rephrase a passage enhances learning tremendously, and the teacher could gain a valuable insight into the language structures the children actually use.

Research findings on producing readable writing

We have looked briefly at two important aspects of rewriting: the curriculum context and children's perceptions. We turn now to some of the insights which have been gleaned by researchers into text difficulties. Perhaps one should stress again that the literature on verbal learning is great, and that the intention here is to draw out general conclusions; this summary is therefore inevitably idiosyncratic. The research findings are grouped under three headings: vocabulary, syntax, and other factors.

Vocabulary

It has been shown consistently that vocabulary is the single factor most closely associated with difficulty in a passage, but this does not mean that it is an easy variable to manipulate. Initially, we might feel that two large classes of words are not really amenable to simplification or alteration: these are (i) words which serve a solely grammatical function, such as *the* or *in*, and (ii) words which have a precise and unavoidable semantic function, such as technical terms, names of substances and so on. Nevertheless, it would be premature to dismiss either possibility. The second point turns on the adjective *unavoidable*. One of the features of the English language is that it is extremely rich in synonyms, so that far fewer words are irreplaceable than would be the case in some other languages.

In an admirable 50-page monograph, George Klare (1975b) offers authors a manual for readable writing, and in it he gives a list of six vocabulary factors which can make a text easier to read and understand. Each point is substantiated by reference to between three and six research studies or reports. The list is worth reproducing in full:

1. *Word frequency and familiarity*. Words of high (versus low) frequency and/or familiarity contribute to more readable writing; found for nouns particularly, but also for other content words. Compare *meal* with *repast*, *household* with *menage*, *leave* with *depart*, *count* with *reckon*.

2. *Word length*. Shorter words (versus longer) tend to make writing more readable; generally found for content words, but sometimes also for function words. Examples are *owner* versus *proprietor*, *go* versus *proceed*, *bloody* versus *sanguinary*, *too* versus *additionally*.

3. *Association value*. Words which call up other words quickly and easily add to readability of writing more than those which do not; studies made with nouns chiefly, but several with adjectives. *Girl* brings *boy* to mind more quickly than *man*, *hand* suggests *foot* sooner than *leg*, and *sleepy* suggests *drowsy* before *heavy*: *love* calls up associations more easily than *amour*, and *law* more quickly than *decree*.

4. *Concreteness–abstractness*. Concrete words, which easily arouse an image in one's mind, contribute more to readable writing than words which do not (abstract words); studies made with nouns. Winston Churchill must have known instinctively about this; he chose *blood, sweat, toil* and *tears* over something like *bravery, energy,* and *sadness*. Some politicians like to use abstract words like *victory* and *heroism*, whereas their hearers are more likely to visualize and remember *village* and *hospital*. But the difference is easy to miss: *time* is abstract while *timepiece* (or *clock*) is concrete. Adjectives have been scaled for the related quality of vividness. *Savage* is more vivid than *heartless*, for example, and *filthy* than *soiled*.

5. *Active verbs versus nominalizations*. The active verb form tends to make writing more readable than the nominalized form; nominalizations are words (usually verbs) made into noun form. *Consider* may thus become *the consideration of, oppose* become *the opposition to*, or *suppose* become *the supposition that*.

6. *Pronouns and other anaphora*. Anaphora are words or phrases which refer back to a previous word or unit of text; both clarifying what they refer to and limiting their use help to make writing more readable (more research evidence is needed however).
   Examples of anaphora, besides pronouns such as *he* and *she* or *that* and *which*, are phrases like *the above* or *defined earlier* or *in the third paragraph*.

For readers not familiar with linguistics, a comment on Klare's sixth point is perhaps necessary. Anaphoric reference is a necessary part of fluent writing; it saves an intolerable amount of repetition, but it can also cause problems. If a teacher writes *These may contain a variety of liquid foods*, the word *these* has an anaphoric function. The child needs to know to which of the nouns mentioned earlier the demonstrative pronoun refers. If the preceding sentences contained a number of nouns or noun phrases the decision could be very difficult, and in such a case it would help the reader if the original noun was repeated, as for example in *These tubes may contain a variety of liquid foods*. Authors should therefore avoid both too much anaphora, and also too great a distance between the anaphoric pronoun and the original word to which it refers.

If a technical term cannot be avoided or rendered more simply then an author can consider putting a definition next to the word, in the margin or in brackets. The problem for the teacher is to prevent the child simply by-passing the term and reading the gloss, thus missing an opportunity to become more familiar with it. Foreign language teachers are aware of this danger, and many would discourage students from writing too freely in their mother tongue on a literature text, because the tendency would be to read only a mother-tongue version. Nevertheless, in the case of a technical term, a gloss is often preferable to no assistance. Readers need to use the technical term in their own writing, and thus become more familiar with its use. This will save the children from becoming familiar only with the simpler form of expression.

Syntactic variables

In Chapter 1 we noted that five syntactic variables seemed to be associated with difficulties for the reader. They were:

(i) passive verb constructions
(ii) nominalisations used where an active verb would suffice
(iii) large numbers of subordinate clauses
(iv) large numbers of modal verbs (*might, would, could*, etc.)
(v) compressions and substitutions

As John Dawkins demonstrated in his book, *Syntax and Readability* (1975), much of the research into syntax has been undertaken by specialists in linguistics rather than specialists in education, and this means that there has been more research about how we process sentences than on how we learn from them. With reference to the research into the comprehension of passives, two points emerge which interest us as teachers: generally speaking, it is harder to judge correctly whether a sentence is true or false if it is presented in the passive voice, and a student will find it harder to recall the context of a sentence if it is presented in the passive voice. Why should this be? It could be that our natural preference is to test the truth value of active-voice statements, and we thus have to operate on the passive sentence before we can test its truth value, which in turn allows the possibility of error in the transformation. Alternatively, it could be that we are much more familiar with active constructions, and that we therefore understand more readily constructions which best fit our expectations.

Many science teachers might suggest that passive constructions are an important part of the special linguistic field of science writing, and it is simply coincidental that difficult concepts and passive constructions occur together, resulting in an unfortunate slur on the passive form. The experiments into verbal learning do not support this view, however. Researchers normally try to find reversible passive sentences, in which there is no content bias towards either form, and in which the ideas themselves are not difficult, such as *The cat saw the dog*. It is on the basis of research into the processing of this kind of sentence that it has been found that passives are more difficult to recall or understand, so there would appear to be some justification for limiting their use, particularly in self-instructional materials. Of course, the human brain does not function in a way which obeys the formal rules of transformational grammar. We now know that some of the psychological experiments undertaken during the 1960s were based on an oversimplified view of Chomsky's theories, and that in any event there are some passive constructions which are easier to comprehend than their active transformations. As Kintsch (1974, p. 313) has argued, the comprehender is not a transformational grammarian in disguise; the reader's aim is to construct meaning, not to perform a syntactic analysis.

This line of argument would lead us to put additional weight on the other explanation of difficulty of processing passives, namely their unfamiliarity. Trabasso (1972) has reported that given a free response situation, even articulate subjects will be twenty times more likely to describe a photograph using the active voice than the passive. As with vocabulary, therefore, it would appear that a construction's frequency of use is a good predictor of its comprehensibility. We could liken a reader's search for sentence meaning with the word-recognition process in a fluent reader. Normally the small amount of information picked up from a feature analysis of parts of a word will suffice, particularly if the meaning is compatible with the preceding context. If a reader encounters an anomolous meaning, or cannot predict any meaning, the word will be scanned again and processed more fully at the graphic, and morphemic or 'sememic' levels, i.e. at the level of single letters, while searching for the smallest units of meaning. Similarly, given a simple sentence, we hardly notice the grammatical constraints, and key semantic elements (e.g. *dog*, *steak*, and *eaten*) are sufficient to ensure comprehension. Only when more complex or less familiar content is encountered do we undertake some kind of syntactic analysis.

The second point, concerning nominalisations, was also included by Klare in his list of vocabulary factors, and this is perfectly reasonable. The factor may also be described as a syntactic variable in that the active verb rendering will take the form of a clause rather than a single noun. The value in preferring the active verb form is in its greater concreteness of meaning. Consider our example from Chapter 1: *The reduction in the length* . . . becomes *If you reduce the length* . . . This has the effect of making the information more immediately related to a person and also to a physical action. The importance of personal reference is one to which we shall return in the next subsection.

We know that a large number of subordinate clauses per sentence, and long subordinate clauses are both associated with difficulties in comprehension. In the case of such sentences, however, no straightforward guidelines for simplification can be offered. We know that breaking up long periodic sentences (for example those with main clauses joined by *and*) will not do much to lower difficulty, because the clauses are structurally separate to begin with. We also know that in some cases splitting up complex sentences can make a text easier to understand, but there can be dangers in attempting this, as we saw in the examples at the beginning of this chapter.

The problem is that syntactic complexity is not independent of conceptual difficulty, or at least only rarely. Modal verbs, for example, increase grammatical complexity only slightly, but they can have a crucial effect on meaning. The use of such verb forms (for example *might, could, may* or *should*) is much more than a stylistic variation. In his description of the differences between the thinking of a junior-school child and an adolescent, Jean Piaget stresses that one of the most important things the older child can do is to subordinate reality to possibility, that is, to take account of what *might be*, rather than what *is*. In the language of formal logic it is possible to express the concept of possibility in mathematical terms, with the concepts of possibility and necessity being represented by symbols which can be used as operators to affect the truth value of a proposition. In contrast to passive sentences, however, it is not usually possible to remove the modal verb without changing the meaning.

Modal verbs are associated with 'vagueness' in the next subsection, but they appear generally to be too deeply embedded in the semantic framework of their sentences to be readily removed or replaced.

Our final point relates to compression and substitution. If clause length is reduced by introducing too much compression the resulting prose could be more difficult than the original, and linguistics research abounds with incomprehensible sentences to demonstrate the point.

Although syntax is known to be a factor on which it is difficult to offer specific guidelines for authors, at least we can be aware of the fact. In judging this aspect of texts, therefore, we should place a relatively greater value on the importance of comments and opinions from colleagues and the students who are to be using the texts.

Other factors

One of the most interesting short studies giving information about other factors which can make texts more comprehensible is not new; it is a paper given by Barak Rosenshine in 1968 to the International Reading Association. He reported a number of studies in which researchers considered aspects of printed texts and spoken lectures to which a normal readability formula is not sensitive. These were the main findings which he reported.

(i) *Organisation*. When two groups of students were given passages from social studies textbooks, one set of which was rewritten in order to make the organisation of the information more clear, the group using the 'organised' versions obtained significantly higher scores on a common test based on the original material.

(ii) *Human interest*. A similar effect was found for passages which were rewritten in order to include more 'human interest'. This factor has been variously defined, but for our purposes we can consider it to imply more direct addressing of the reader, especially by using the 'you' form, and more specific references to people and their actions and concerns. Not every occurrence of a personal pronoun would count as a personal reference, and therefore as a token of human interest; in some scientific or expository prose the 'we' form is common, but is used in such a manner for editorial purposes rather than to increase human interest.

(iii) *Avoiding vagueness*. Vagueness, defined as 'a writing style characterised by an excessive proportion of qualification, haziness and ambiguity' was found to be one factor associated with poor comprehensibility. In particular 'probability words' and 'indeterminate qualifiers' such as *rather, very, more or less, few, some, pretty much*, and *quite a bit* were pinpointed as factors contributing to an impression of vagueness. [As an impenitent user of probability words and indeterminate qualifiers, I would protest that such words are necessary in any field in which accurate expression is important, and thus that such words are a natural concomitant of both literary and scientific prose. No doubt such qualifiers increase the reader's information processing load, and they should sometimes be avoided, but it would be difficult to eradicate them entirely. Rosenshine's own prose is peppered with indeterminate qualifiers to such an extent that he rather damages his own case, as a brief quotation shows: '. . . although the use of short words *usually* correlates positively with the reading ease, there are *some very* short words which *more often than not*, might *possibly* detract *very much* from readability'. Rosenshine's prose is in fact clear and readable, and although he uses many qualifiers the overall impression is not one of vagueness, but this is as much due to his careful organisation as much as anything else.]

(iv) *Explaining links*. Adverbs and conjunctions such as *therefore, because, consequently*, and *since* were found to be more helpful for students than the simple conjunctions *and* or *but*. Clearly their effect is to turn a statement into an 'explaining sentence', and children could be taught to give special attention to such sentences. Introducing explaining links where appropriate could be one way of clarifying the organisation of passage content which was suggested as important in subsection (i).

(v) *Rule and example*. The time-honoured triptychs of *precept-example-restatement* or *general point-examples-summary* were used by lecturers whose students had good recall of lecture content. The less effective relied on only one summary statement, and this was usually presented before the series of examples, rather than after it.

(vi) *Avoiding irrelevancy*. This was a tantalising finding: although redundancy was found to be effective in increasing learning (in other words the more examples the better), it was discovered that, overall, the shortest lectures were the ones which were best remembered. Such a finding will give all teachers food for thought.

Implications

The previous section has offered at least a few suggestions about writing more readable prose. The suggestions are not prescriptions, because the skill of writing clearly is not something which can be governed by prescription; it is an art rather than a science. Readers who wish to read more about learning from printed materials would do well to consult the excellent *Bibliography for Textual Communication* produced by MacDonald-Ross and Smith (1973). This lists over 800 references in fields as diverse as information science, programmed learning, content analysis and technical writing, and gives a much broader view of textual design than would be appropriate here.

If writers – whether professional authors or classroom teachers – wish to produce more readable writing, they must take three groups of factors into account. These are the context within which the text will be read and used, the nature and likely competence of the audience, and their own vocabulary and style. From the teacher's point of view in writing or evaluating materials, the curriculum context, though crucial, is the factor on which he has to make a necessarily subjective judgment. Most teachers are eclectic, and their use of resources will vary widely from school to school. The second factor, the readers' competence, is one for which objective data can supplement personal judgment: in particular, we have suggested that students' performance, their own opinions, and the careful use of cloze testing, can give the teacher valuable information about how another class is likely to cope with a worksheet or book. The third group of factors, those connected with prose style, are not always amenable to systematic or reliable measurement. In Bormuth's extensive study (1969a) of the relationship between over 160 language variables and reading comprehension, many constructions occurred so infrequently that no clear pattern of correlation could emerge. This is why a readability formula based on just two variables, word length and sentence length, can often be more valuable. Crude though it appears, it can actually give a far better indication of probable difficulty than a multi-variable formula, since every extra variable is contributing less and less to the overall predictive accuracy, but is introducing an extra possibility of error.

Provided, therefore, that we remember the important point that formulae should be applied *post hoc*, and not used as a prescription, we can use readability scores as an additional source of information at the redaction or revision stage. There have been some inconclusive studies of readability and comprehension, but three points do stand out:

—Generally speaking, and especially when reading time is controlled, passages with a lower readability score are better understood than comparable passages with a higher score (Klare, 1975b):
—Given a chance to state an opinion, readers prefer to read easier

prose, and this is true for good readers as well as poor readers (Klare, 1963, p. 141):
— In 'free reading' (notably with journals, magazines and correspondence courses) the level of readability may play a significant role in encouraging or discouraging the reader (Klare, 1963).

Conclusion

Professional responsibility should be a prime consideration in the use of readability measures. As we have stressed from the outset, it is misleading and even potentially harmful to misuse readability data. The following brief checklist can help to ensure that such data is used responsibly:

Validity: Is the text written in sentences, and in either narrative or expository prose? If not, it may be invalid to use a formula.

Reliability: Is the chosen formula appropriate for the age-group under consideration?

   Is a large enough text sample being analysed?

   Are counts of syllables, etc., to be double-checked for accuracy?

Utility: Is allowance to be made for the effect of level of readers' motivation (be it high or low)?

   Is the information to be shared with colleagues?

   What teaching strategies are to be adopted in the event of a mismatch between text and potential audience?

These questions relate to one aspect of professional responsibility – the use to which readability formulae are put – but there is a wider issue, namely that of who is responsible for the overall level of readability of school materials. Most teachers will accept the responsibility for their own worksheets, but what about textbooks? It is normal for teachers to make the assumption that publishers are responsible for the comprehensibility or otherwise of the textbooks in our schools, but another view is tenable. The standard argument that we can only buy what the educational publishers put on their lists is an insubstantial one. Publishers will only retain on their lists books and courses which sell, and this means that it is the teachers who ultimately have the power to determine what stays on the list, and therefore what can be bought into the department as a textbook. Teachers have the power to determine the readability of textbooks, and they must also accept the responsibility which is the concomitant of that power.

The suggestion being made here is that as teachers we have been neglectful rather than irresponsible; that content and presentation have been the determinants of selection to the exclusion of factors related to readability, and that this in turn has resulted in greater dependence on teacher-exegesis and fewer possibilities for children's self-directed learning. Evaluation of our own courses is becoming more widely accepted as a major professional responsibility, and assessing printed materials must be a part of such an undertaking. This is not a call for indiscriminate readability testing of every scrap of paper in the school. It is rather a reminder that if we do not become better at evaluating ourselves, the accountability movement will be likely to do the job for us. Every department should surely be in a position to answer the question 'How well can your children cope with the reading material they handle?' and yet, as we saw in Chapter 1, as individuals we are not very reliable judges of text difficulty. One answer to this may certainly be to systematise the pooling and sharing of teachers' subjective judgments and experience, but another is to make judicious use of the objective data to which we can have access, whether it is based on a measure of pupils' responses or on a readability index.

The history of readability measurement in the United States shows periods of activity erupting in different decades since the 1920s. It appears that in the United Kingdom there is likely to be a surge of interest in readability work, which can be related to curriculum development in the language field which has followed the publication of the Bullock report. Many schools have used formula scores as a part of in-service work within their own staff-development courses, and it is likely that this will continue. If readability data can assist in the task of raising the level of consciousness within a staffroom about the difficulties children face in coping with print in different subject areas, then it will have served a useful purpose. Nevertheless, readability measures can be used in a more direct way, in helping to match readers to suitable texts. Providing a formula score is never used to deny children access to what they wish to read, this use of readability data might be profitably extended, particularly in subjects where motivation to read is low.

Even if a teacher has access to a computerised readability score, gathering such data is going to take time and effort, and it is important that these are not wasted. One would hope, therefore, to see an extension of the kind of information exchange run by the National Association for Remedial Education and the United Kingdom Reading Association. Both these organisations circulate to members lists of readability results on a large number of books, and it would be valuable if other subject associations and professional groups collaborated in a similar manner to avoid duplication of effort. Educational publishers are understandably wary about printing readability scores on their books. Teachers feel that this is because of an anxiety that they would restrict or depress sales, but there is a genuine concern that the data would be misused. The largest UK educational publisher found that teachers were sadly ill-equipped to cope with Dewey classification numbers when these were printed on their books, and they blench at the thought of what most teachers would make of a readability score. Many publishers do in fact use readability data but choose not to publicise the results becuase they feel teachers would take the scores to represent an exact reading level rather than a general indication.

One task which remains to be done is to establish age level norms for a British readability index. In one sense this is not vital: the American formulae are valid in the United Kingdom; the Schools Council Effective Use of Reading project was one of a number of studies which have demonstrated that this is so. However, there is no formula in which the age levels were derived from the performance of a large group of UK children. At present, confidence in applying US formulae in the UK is grounded in the high correlations between pooled teacher judgments and the formulae scores. These do not fix the age level, though. Broadly speaking the performance of UK and US children is parallel over age-groups, but cross-cultural comparisons are notoriously difficult, and only when this important and formidable research task is tackled shall UK teachers have a basis for reliability which is as solid as that of the most rigorous formulae produced in the United States.

Appendix A
Dale's 3,000 word list

a
able
aboard
about
above
absent
accept
accident
account
ache(ing)
acorn
acre
across
act(s)
add
address
admire
adventure
afar
afraid
after
afternoon
afterward(s)
again
against
age
aged
ago
agree
ah
ahead
aid
aim
air
airfield
airplane
airport
airship
airy
alarm
alike
alive
all
alley
alligator
allow
almost
alone
along
aloud
already
also
always
am
America
American
among

amount
an
and
angel
anger
angry
animal
another
answer
ant
any
anybody
anyhow
anyone
anything
anyway
anywhere
apart
apartment
ape
apiece
appear
apple
April
apron
are
aren't
arise
arithmetic
arm
armful
army
arose
around
arrange
arrive(d)
arrow
art
artist
as
ash(es)
aside
ask
asleep
at
ate
attack
attend
attention
August
aunt
author
auto
automobile
autumn
avenue
awake(n)

away
awful(ly)
awhile
ax

baa
babe
baby(ies)
back
background
backward(s)
bacon
bad(ly)
badge
bag
bake(r)
bakery
baking
ball
balloon
banana
band
bandage
bang
banjo
bank(er)
bar
barber
bare(ly)
barefoot
bark
barn
barrel
base
baseball
basement
basket
bat
batch
bath
bathe
bathing
bathroom
bathtub
battle
battleship
bay
be(ing)
beach
bead
beam
bean
bear
beard
beast
beat(ing)
beautiful

beautify
beauty
became
because
become
becoming
bed
bedbug
bedroom
bedspread
bedtime
bee
beech
beef
beefsteak
beehive
been
beer
beet
before
beg
began
beggar
begged
begin
beginning
begun
behave
behind
believe
bell
belong
below
belt
bench
bend
beneath
bent
berry(ies)
beside(s)
best
bet
better
between
bib
bible
bicycle
bid
big(ger)
bill
billboard
bin
bind
bird
birth
birthday
biscuit

bit
bite
biting
bitter
black
blackberry
blackbird
blackboard
blackness
blacksmith
blame
blank
blanket
blast
blaze
bleed
bless
blessing
blew
blind(s)
blindfold
block
blood
bloom
blossom
blot
blow
blue
blueberry
bluejay
blush
board
boast
boat
bob
bobwhite
body(ies)
boil(er)
bold
bone
bonnet
boo
book
bookcase
bookkeeper
boom
boot
born
borrow
boss
both
bother
bottle
bottom
bought
bounce

bow
bowl
bow-wow
box(es)
boxcar
boxer
boy
boyhood
bracelet
brain
brake
bran
branch
brass
brave
bread
break
breakfast
breast
breath
breathe
breeze
brick
bride
bridge
bright
brightness
bring
broad
broadcast
broke(n)
brook
broom
brother
brought
brown
brush
bubble
bucket
buckle
bud
buffalo
bug
buggy
build
building
built
bulb
bull
bullet
bum
bumblebee
bump
bun
bunch
bundle
bunny

burn
burst
bury
bus
bush
bushel
business
busy
but
butcher
butt
butter
buttercup
butterfly
buttermilk
butterscotch
button
buttonhole
buy
buzz
by
bye

cab
cabbage
cabin
cabinet
cackle
cage
cake
calendar
calf
call(er)(ing)
came
camel
camp
campfire
can
canal
canary
candle
candlestick
candy
cane
cannon
cannot
canoe
can't
canyon
cap
cape
capital
captain
car
card
cardboard
care

153

careful	childhood	cocoon	cramps	dart	do	dwarf
careless	children	cod	cranberry	dash	dock	dwell
carelessness	chill(y)	codfish	crank(y)	date	doctor	dwelt
carload	chimney	coffee	crash	daughter	does	dying
carpenter	chin	coffeepot	crawl	dawn	doesn't	
carpet	china	coin	crazy	day	dog	each
carriage	chip	cold	cream(y)	daybreak	doll	eager
carrot	chipmunk	collar	creek	daytime	dollar	eagle
carry	chocolate	college	creep	dead	dolly	ear
cart	choice	color(ed)	crept	deaf	done	early
carve	choose	colt	cried	deal	donkey	earn
case	chop	column	croak	dear	don't	earth
cash	chorus	comb	crook(ed)	death	door	east(ern)
cashier	chose(n)	come	crop	December	doorbell	easy
castle	christen	comfort	cross(ing)	decide	doorknob	eat(en)
cat	Christmas	comic	cross-eyed	deck	doorstep	edge
catbird	church	coming	crow	deed	dope	egg
catch	churn	company	crowd(ed)	deep	dot	eh
catcher	cigarette	compare	crown	deer	double	eight
caterpillar	circle	conductor	cruel	defeat	dough	eighteen
catfish	circus	cone	crumb	defend	dove	eighth
catsup	citizen	connect	crumble	defense	down	eighty
cattle	city	coo	crush	delight	downstairs	either
caught	clang	cook(ed)	crust	den	downtown	elbow
cause	clap	cook(ing)	cry(ies)	dentist	dozen	elder
cave	class	cooky(ie)(s)	cub	depend	drag	eldest
ceiling	classmate	cool(er)	cuff	deposit	drain	electric
cell	classroom	coop	cup	describe	drank	electricity
cellar	claw	copper	cupboard	desert	draw(er)	elephant
cent	clay	copy	cupful	deserve	draw(ing)	eleven
center	clean(er)	cord	cure	desire	dream	elf
cereal	clear	cork	curl(y)	desk	dress	elm
certain(ly)	clerk	corn	curtain	destroy	dresser	else
chain	clever	corner	curve	devil	dressmaker	elsewhere
chair	click	correct	cushion	dew	drew	empty
chalk	cliff	cost	custard	diamond	dried	end(ing)
champion	climb	cot	customer	did	drift	enemy
chance	clip	cottage	cut	didn't	drill	engine
change	cloak	cotton	cute	die(d)(s)	drink	engineer
chap	clock	couch	cutting	difference	drip	English
charge	close	cough		different	drive(n)	enjoy
charm	closet	could	dab	dig	driver	enough
chart	cloth	couldn't	dad	dim	drop	enter
chase	clothes	count	daddy	dime	drove	envelope
chatter	clothing	counter	daily	dine	drown	equal
cheap	cloud(y)	country	dairy	ding-dong	drowsy	erase(r)
cheat	clover	county	daisy	dinner	drug	errand
check	clown	course	dam	dip	drum	escape
checkers	club	court	damage	direct	drunk	eve
check	cluck	cousin	dame	direction	dry	even
cheer	clump	cover	damp	dirt(y)	duck	evening
cheese	coach	cow	dance(r)	discover	due	ever
cherry	coal	coward(ly)	dancing	dish	dug	every
chest	coast	cowboy	dandy	dislike	dull	everybody
chew	coat	cozy	danger(ous)	dismiss	dumb	everyday
chick	cob	crab	dare	ditch	dump	everyone
chicken	cobbler	crack	dark(ness)	dive	during	everything
chief	cocoa	cracker	darling	diver	dust(y)	everywhere
child	coconut	cradle	darn	divide	duty	evil

exact	fiddle	follow(ing)	gain	gown	ham	hello
except	field	fond	gallon	grab	hammer	helmet
exchange	fife	food	gallop	gracious	hand	help(er)
excited	fifteen	fool	game	grade	handful	helpful
exciting	fifth	foolish	gang	grain	handker-	hem
excuse	fifty	foot	garage	grand	chief	hen
exit	fig	football	garbage	grandchild	handle	henhouse
expect	fight	footprint	garden	grandchildren	handwrit-	her(s)
explain	figure	for	gas	granddaughter	ing	herd
extra	file	forehead	gasoline	grandfather	hang	here
eye	fill	forest	gate	grandma	happen	here's
eyebrow	film	forget	gather	grandmother	happily	hero
	finally	forgive	gave	grandpa	happiness	herself
fable	find	forgot(ten)	gay	grandson	happy	he's
face	fine	fork	gear	grandstand	harbor	hey
facing	finger	form	geese	grape(s)	hard	hickory
fact	finish	fort	general	grapefruit	hardly	hid
factory	fire	forth	gentle	grass	hardship	hidden
fail	firearm	fortune	gentleman	grasshopper	hardware	hide
faint	firecracker	forty	gentlemen	grateful	hare	high
fair	fireplace	forward	geography	grave	hark	highway
fairy	fireworks	fought	get	gravel	harm	hill
faith	firing	found	getting	graveyard	harness	hillside
fake	first	fountain	giant	gravy	harp	hilltop
fall	fish	four	gift	gray	harvest	hilly
false	fisherman	fourteen	gingerbread	graze	has	him
family	fist	fourth	girl	grease	hasn't	himself
fan	fit(s)	fox	give(n)	great	haste(n)	hind
fancy	five	frame	giving	green	hasty	hint
far	fix	free	glad(ly)	greet	hat	hip
faraway	flag	freedom	glance	grew	hatch	hire
fare	flake	freeze	glass(es)	grind	hatchet	his
farmer	flame	freight	gleam	groan	hate	hiss
farm(ing)	flap	French	glide	grocery	haul	history
far-off	flash	fresh	glory	ground	have	hit
farther	flashlight	fret	glove	group	haven't	hitch
fashion	flat	Friday	glow	grove	having	hive
fast	flea	fried	glue	grow	hawk	ho
fasten	flesh	friend(ly)	go(ing)	guard	hay	hoe
fat	flew	friendship	goes	guess	hayfield	hog
father	flies	frighten	goal	guest	haystack	hold(er)
fault	flight	frog	goat	guide	he	hole
favor	flip	from	gobble	gulf	head	holiday
favorite	flip-flop	front	God(g)	gum	headache	hollow
fear	float	frost	godmother	gun	heal	holy
feast	flock	frown	gold(en)	gunpowder	health(y)	home
feather	flood	froze	goldfish	guy	heap	homely
February	floor	fruit	golf		hear(ing)	homesick
fed	flop	fry	gone	ha	heard	honest
feed	flour	fudge	good(s)	habit	heart	honey
feel	flow	fuel	good-by(bye)	had	heat(er)	honeybee
feet	flower(y)	full(y)	good-looking	hadn't	heaven	honeymoon
fell	flutter	fun	goodness	hail	heavy	honk
fellow	fly	funny	goody	hair	he'd	honor
felt	foam	fur	goose	haircut	heel	hood
fence	fog	furniture	gooseberry	hairpin	height	hoof
fever	foggy	further	got	half	held	hook
few	fold	fuzzy	govern	hall	hell	hoop
fib	folks		government	halt	he'll	hop

hope(ful)	ink	kettle	leap	lonesome	matter	mop
hopeless	inn	key	learn(ed)	long	mattress	more
horn	insect	kick	least	look	may(M)	morning
horse	inside	kid	leather	lookout	maybe	morrow
horseback	instant	kill(ed)	leave(ing)	loop	mayor	moss
horseshoe	instead	kind(ly)	led	loose	maypole	most(ly)
hose	insult	kindness	left	lord	me	mother
hospital	intend	king	leg	lose(r)	meadow	motor
host	interested	kingdom	lemon	loss	meal	mount
hot	interesting	kiss	lemonade	lost	mean(s)	mountain
hotel	into	kitchen	lend	lot	meant	mouse
hound	invite	kite	length	loud	measure	mouth
hour	iron	kitten	less	love	meat	move
house	is	kitty	lesson	lovely	medicine	movie
housetop	island	knee	let	lover	meet(ing)	movies
housewife	isn't	kneel	let's	low	melt	moving
housework	it	knew	letter	luck(y)	member	mow
how	its	knife	letting	lumber	men	Mr., Mrs.
however	it's	knit	lettuce	lump	mend	much
howl	itself	knives	level	lunch	meow	mud
hug	I've	knob	liberty	lying	merry	muddy
huge	ivory	knock	library		mess	mug
hum	ivy	knot	lice	ma	message	mule
humble		know	lick	machine	met	multiply
hump	jacket	known	lid	machinery	metal	murder
hundred	jacks		lie	mad	mew	music
hung	jail	lace	life	made	mice	must
hunger	jam	lad	lift	magazine	middle	my
hungry	January	ladder	light(ness)	magic	midnight	myself
hunk	jar	ladies	lightning	maid	might(y)	
hunt(er)	jaw	lady	like	mail	mile	nail
hurrah	jay	laid	likely	mailbox	milk	name
hurried	jelly	lake	liking	mailman	milkman	nap
hurry	jellyfish	lamb	lily	major	mill	napkin
hurt	jerk	lame	limb	make	miller	narrow
husband	jig	lamp	lime	making	million	nasty
hush	job	land	limp	male	mind	naughty
hut	jockey	lane	line	mama	mine	navy
hymn	join	language	linen	mamma	miner	near
	joke	lantern	lion	man	mint	nearby
I	joking	lap	lip	manager	minute	nearly
ice	jolly	lard	list	mane	mirror	neat
icy	journey	large	listen	manger	mischief	neck
I'd	joy(ful)	lash	lit	many	miss(M)	necktie
idea	joyous	lass	little	map	misspell	need
ideal	judge	last	live(s)	maple	mistake	needle
if	jug	late	lively	marble	misty	needn't
ill	juice	laugh	liver	march(M)	mitt	Negro
I'll	juicy	laundry	living	mare	mitten	neighbor
I'm	July	law	lizard	mark	mix	neighborhood
important	jump	lawn	load	market	moment	neither
impossible	June	lawyer	loaf	marriage	Monday	nerve
improve	junior	lay	loan	married	money	nest
in	junk	lazy	loaves	marry	monkey	net
inch(es)	just	lead	lock	mask	month	never
income		leader	locomotive	mast	moo	nevermore
indeed	keen	leaf	log	master	moon	new
Indian	keep	leak	lone	mat	moonlight	news
indoors	kept	lean	lonely	match	moose	newspaper

next	orchard	partner	pit	present	rainbow	ring
nibble	order	party	pitch	pretty	raise	rip
nice	ore	pass	pitcher	price	raisin	ripe
nickel	organ	passenger	pity	prick	rake	rise
night	other	past	place	prince	ram	rising
nightgown	otherwise	paste	plain	princess	ran	river
nine	ouch	pasture	plan	print	ranch	road
nineteen	ought	pat	plane	prison	rang	roadside
ninety	our(s)	patch	plant	prize	rap	roar
no	ourselves	path	plate	promise	rapidly	roast
nobody	out	patter	platform	proper	rat	rob
nod	outdoors	pave	platter	protect	rate	robber
noise	outfit	pavement	play(er)	proud	rather	robe
noisy	outlaw	paw	playground	prove	rattle	robin
none	outline	pay	playhouse	prune	raw	rock(y)
noon	outside	payment	playmate	public	ray	rocket
nor	outward	pea(s)	plaything	puddle	reach	rode
north(ern)	oven	peace(ful)	pleasant	puff	read	roll
nose	over	peach(es)	please	pull	reader	roller
not	overalls	peak	pleasure	pump	reading	roof
note	overcoat	peanut	plenty	pumpkin	ready	room
nothing	overeat	pear	plow	punch	real	rooster
notice	overhead	pearl	plug	punish	really	root
November	overhear	peck	plum	pup	reap	rope
now	overnight	peek	pocket	pupil	rear	rose
nowhere	overturn	peel	pocketbook	puppy	reason	rosebud
number	owe	peep	poem	pure	rebuild	rot
nurse	owing	peg	point	purple	receive	rotten
nut	owl	pen	poison	purse	recess	rough
	own(er)	pencil	poke	push	record	round
oak	ox	penny	pole	puss	red	route
oar		people	police	pussy	redbird	row
oatmeal	pa	pepper	policeman	pussycat	redbreast	rowboat
oats	pace	peppermint	polish	put	refuse	royal
obey	pack	perfume	polite	putting	reindeer	rub
ocean	package	perhaps	pond	puzzle	rejoice	rubbed
o'clock	pad	person	ponies		remain	rubber
October	page	pet	pony	quack	remember	rubbish
odd	paid	phone	pool	quart	remind	rug
of	pail	piano	poor	quarter	remove	rule(r)
off	pain(ful)	pick	pop	queen	rent	rumble
offer	paint(er)	pickle	popcorn	queer	repair	run
office	painting	picnic	popped	question	repay	rung
officer	pair	picture	porch	quick(ly)	repeat	runner
often	pal	pie	pork	quiet	report	running
oh	palace	piece	possible	quilt	rest	rush
oil	pale	pig	post	quit	return	rust(y)
old	pan	pigeon	postage	quite	review	rye
old-	pancake	piggy	postman		reward	
fashioned	pane	pile	pot	rabbit	rib	sack
on	pansy	pill	potato(es)	race	ribbon	sad
once	pants	pillow	pound	rack	rice	saddle
one	papa	pin	pour	radio	rich	sadness
onion	paper	pine	powder	radish	rid	safe
only	parade	pineapple	power(ful)	rag	riddle	safety
onward	pardon	pink	praise	rail	ride(r)	said
open	parent	pint	pray	railroad	riding	sail
or	park	pipe	prayer	railway	right	sailboat
orange	part(ly)	pistol	prepare	rain(y)	rim	sailor

saint	sent	shout	slipped	speak(er)	sting	surprise
salad	sentence	shovel	slipper	spear	stir	swallow
sale	separate	show	slippery	speech	stitch	swam
salt	September	shower	slit	speed	stock	swamp
same	servant	shut	slow(ly)	spell(ing)	stocking	swan
sand(y)	serve	shy	sly	spend	stole	swat
sandwich	service	sick(ness)	smack	spent	stone	swear
sang	set	side	small	spider	stood	sweat
sank	setting	sidewalk	smart	spike	stool	sweater
sap	settle	sideways	smell	spill	stoop	sweep
sash	settlement	sigh	smile	spin	stop	sweet(ness)
sat	seven	sight	smoke	spinach	stopped	sweetheart
satin	seventeen	sign	smooth	spirit	stopping	swell
satisfactory	seventh	silence	snail	spit	store	swept
Saturday	seventy	silent	snake	splash	stories	swift
sausage	several	silk	snap	spoil	stork	swim
savage	sew	sill	snapping	spoke	storm(y)	swimming
save	shade	silly	sneeze	spook	story	swing
savings	shadow	silver	snow(y)	spoon	stove	switch
saw	shady	simple	snowball	sport	straight	sword
say	shake(r)	sin	snowflake	spot	strange(r)	swore
scab	shaking	since	snuff	spread	strap	
scales	shall	sing	snug	spring	straw	table
scare	shame	singer	so	springtime	strawberry	tablecloth
scarf	shan't	single	soak	sprinkle	stream	tablespoon
school	shape	sink	soap	square	street	tablet
schoolboy	share	sip	sob	squash	stretch	tack
schoolhouse	sharp	sir	socks	squeak	string	tag
schoolmaster	shave	sis	sod	squeeze	strip	tail
schoolroom	she	sissy	soda	squirrel	stripes	tailor
scorch	she'd	sister	sofa	stable	strong	take(n)
score	she'll	sit	soft	stack	stuck	taking
scrap	she's	sitting	soil	stage	study	tale
scrape	shear(s)	six	sold	stair	stuff	talk(er)
scratch	shed	sixteen	soldier	stall	stump	tall
scream	sheep	sixth	sole	stamp	stung	tame
screen	sheet	sixty	some	stand	subject	tan
screw	shelf	size	somebody	star	such	tank
scrub	shell	skate	somehow	stare	suck	tap
sea	shepherd	skater	someone	start	sudden	tape
seal	shine	ski	something	starve	suffer	tar
seam	shining	skin	sometime(s)	state	sugar	tardy
search	shiny	skip	somewhere	station	suit	task
season	ship	skirt	son	stay	sum	taste
seat	shirt	sky	song	steak	summer	taught
second	shock	slam	soon	steal	sun	tax
secret	shoe	slap	sore	steam	Sunday	tea
see(ing)	shoemaker	slate	sorrow	steamboat	sunflower	teach(er)
seed	shone	slave	sorry	steamer	sung	team
seek	shook	sled	sort	steel	sunk	tear
seem	shoot	sleep(y)	soul	steep	sunlight	tease
seen	shop	sleeve	sound	steeple	sunny	teaspoon
seesaw	shopping	sleigh	soup	steer	sunrise	teeth
select	shore	slept	sour	stem	sunset	telephone
self	short	slice	south(ern)	step	sunshine	tell
selfish	shot	slid	space	stepping	supper	temper
sell	should	slide	spade	stick(y)	suppose	ten
send	shoulder	sling	spank	stiff	sure(ly)	tennis
sense	shouldn't	slip	sparrow	still(ness)	surface	tent

term
terrible
test
than
thank(s)
thankful
Thanks-
    giving
that
that's
the
theater
thee
their
them
then
there
these
they
they'd
they'll
they're
they've
thick
thief
thimble
thin
thing
think
third
thirsty
thirteen
thirty
this
tho
thorn
those
though
thought
thousand
thread
three
threw
throat
throne
through
throw(n)
thumb
thunder
Thursday
thy
tick
ticket
tickle
tie
tiger
tight
till
time

tin
tinkle
tiny
tip
tiptoe
tire
tired
'tis
title
to
toad
toadstool
toast
tobacco
today
toe
together
toilet
told
tomato
tomorrow
ton
tone
tongue
tonight
too
took
tool
toot
tooth
toothbrush
toothpick
top
tore
torn
toss
touch
tow
toward(s)
towel
tower
town
toy
trace
track
trade
train
tramp
trap
tray
treasure
treat
tree
trick
tricycle
tried
trim
trip
trolley

trouble
truck
true
truly
trunk
trust
truth
try
tub
Tuesday
tug
tulip
tumble
tune
tunnel
turkey
turn
turtle
twelve
twenty
twice
twig
twin
two

ugly
umbrella
uncle
under
understand
underwear
undress
unfair
unfinished
unfold
unfriendly
unhappy
unhurt
uniform
United
    States
unkind
unknown
unless
unpleasant
until
unwilling
up
upon
upper
upset
upside
upstairs
uptown
upward
us
use(d)
useful

valentine
valley
valuable
value
vase
vegetable
velvet
very
vessel
victory
view
village
vine
violet
visit
visitor
voice
vote

wag
wagon
waist
wait
wake(n)
walk
wall
walnut
want
war
warm
warn
was
wash(er)
washtub
wasn't
waste
watch
watchman
water
watermelon
waterproof
wave
wax
way
wayside
we
weak(ness)
weaken
wealth
weapon
wear
weary
weather
weave
web
we'd
wedding
Wednesday
wee

weed
week
weep
weigh
welcome
well
we'll
went
were
we're
west(ern)
wet
we've
whale
what
what's
wheat
wheel
when
whenever
where
which
while
whip
whipped
whirl
whisky
whisper
whistle
white
who
who'd
whole
who'll
whom
who's
whose
why
wicked
wide
wife
wiggle
wild
wildcat
will
willing
willow
win
wind(y)
windmill
window
wine
wing
wink
winner
winter
wipe
wire
wise

wish
wit
witch
with
without
woke
wolf
woman
women
won
wonder
wonderful
won't
wood(en)
woodpecker
woods
wool
woolen
word
wore
work(er)
workman
world
worm
worn
worry
worse
worst
worth
would
wouldn't
wound
wove
wrap
wrapped
wreck
wren
wring
write
writing
written
wrong
wrote
wrung

yard
yarn
year
yell
yellow
yes
yesterday
yet
yolk
yonder
you
you'd
you'll
young

youngster
your(s)
you're
yourself
yourselves
youth
you've

Appendix B
Dale's 769 word list

a	bag	book	catch	cover
about	ball	born	cause	cow
above	band	both	cent	cried
across	bank	bottom	center	cross
act	basket	bow	chair	crowd
afraid	be	box	chance	crown
after	bear	boy	change	cry
afternoon	beat	branch	chief	cup
again	beautiful	brave	child	cut
against	because	bread	children	dance
ago	bed	break	choose	dark
air	bee	breakfast	Christmas	day
all	been	bridge	church	dead
almost	before	bright	circle	dear
alone	began	bring	city	deep
along	begin	broken	class	did
already	behind	brother	clean	die
also	being	brought	clear	different
always	believe	brown	clock	dinner
am	bell	build	close	do
American	belong	building	cloth	doctor
an	beside	built	clothes	does
and	best	burn	cloud	dog
animal	better	busy	coal	done
another	between	but	coat	don't
answer	big	butter	cold	door
any	bill	buy	color	double
anything	bird	by	come	down
apple	bit	cake	coming	draw
are	black	call	company	dream
arm	bless	came	cook	dress
around	blind	can	cool	drink
as	blood	cap	corn	drive
ask	blow	captain	corner	drop
at	blue	car	cost	dry
away	board	care	could	dust
baby	boat	careful	count	each
back	body	carry	country	ear
bad	bone	case	course	early

160

earth	field	go	hill	lake
east	fight	God	him	land
easy	fill	going	himself	large
eat	find	gold	his	last
edge	fine	golden	hold	late
egg	finger	gone	hole	laugh
eight	finish	good	home	lay
either	fire	got	hope	lead
else	first	grain	horse	learn
end	fish	grass	hot	leave
England	fit	gray	house	left
English	five	great	how	leg
enough	fix	green	hundred	lesson
even	floor	grew	hunt	let
evening	flower	ground	hurry	letter
ever	fly	grow	hurt	lie
every	follow	guess	I	lift
everything	food	had	ice	light
except	foot	hair	if	like
expect	for	half	in	line
eye	forget	hall	Indian	lion
face	forth	hand	instead	lips
fair	found	hang	into	listen
fall	four	happy	iron	little
family	fresh	hard	is	live
fancy	friend	has	it	load
far	from	hat	its	long
farm	front	have	jump	look
farmer	fruit	he	just	lost
fast	full	head	keep	lot
fat	game	hear	kept	loud
father	garden	heard	kill	love
feed	gate	heart	kind	low
feel	gave	heavy	king	made
feet	get	help	kiss	mail
fell	gift	her	knee	make
fellow	girl	here	knew	man
felt	give	herself	know	many
fence	glad	hide	lady	march
few	glass	high	laid	mark

market	neighbor	own	ready	send
matter	neither	page	real	sent
may	nest	paint	reason	serve
me	never	pair	red	set
mean	new	paper	remember	seven
measure	New York	part	rest	several
meat	next	party	rich	shake
meet	nice	pass	ride	shall
men	night	path	right	shape
met	nine	pay	ring	she
middle	no	pen	river	sheep
might	noise	people	road	shine
mile	none	pick	rock	ship
milk	noon	picture	roll	shoe
mill	nor	piece	roof	shop
mind	north	place	room	short
mine	nose	plain	rose	should
minute	not	plant	round	shoulder
miss	note	play	row	show
money	nothing	please	run	shut
month	now	point	said	sick
moon	number	poor	sail	side
more	oak	post	salt	sign
morning	ocean	pound	same	silk
most	of	present	sand	silver
mother	off	press	sat	sing
mountain	office	pretty	save	sir
mouth	often	pull	saw	sister
move	old	put	say	sit
Mr.	on	quarter	school	six
Mrs.	once	queen	sea	size
much	one	quick	season	skin
music	only	quiet	seat	sky
must	open	quite	second	sleep
my	or	race	see	slow
myself	other	rain	seed	small
name	our	ran	seem	smile
near	out	rather	seen	smoke
neck	outside	reach	self	snow
need	over	read	sell	so

soft	sure	to	water	work
sold	surprise	today	wave	world
soldier	sweet	together	way	would
some	table	told	we	write
something	tail	tomorrow	wear	wrong
sometime	take	tongue	weather	yard
song	talk	too	week	year
soon	tall	took	well	yellow
sound	taste	top	went	yes
south	teach	touch	were	yesterday
space	teacher	town	west	yet
speak	tear	trade	what	you
spot	tell	train	wheat	young
spread	ten	tree	wheel	your
spring	than	true	when	
square	thank	try	where	
stand	that	turn	whether	
star	the	twelve	which	
start	their	twenty	while	
station	them	two	white	
stay	then	uncle	who	
step	there	under	whole	
stick	these	until	whom	
still	they	up	whose	
stone	thick	upon	why	
stood	thin	us	wide	
stop	thing	use	wild	
store	think	valley	will	
storm	this	very	win	
story	those	visit	wind	
straight	though	wait	window	
street	thought	walk	wing	
strike	thousand	wall	winter	
strong	three	want	wish	
such	through	war	with	
sugar	throw	warm	without	
suit	tie	was	woman	
summer	till	wash	wonder	
sun	time	waste	wood	
suppose	tire (d)	watch	word	

Appendix C
The STAR program for readability estimation

What the program does

The program STAR performs a readability test on data supplied and produces a table of results (indices) using the formulae for measurement outlined below. The indices are derived from linguistic variables in the text (such as the number of syllables per word and the sentence length) and give an estimate (in grade level or age in years) of the readability of the passage(s).

Any number of passages can be analysed in one run. Output for each passage consists of two optional sections, one listing input text and the other listing words of three or more syllables ('hi-cal' words), and a listing of linguistic measures and readability scores.

The readability scores

Different formulae produce different types of measure of text difficulty. The formulae used in the STAR program produce four types of result:

    (a) US school grades
    (b) 'Reading ease' score
    (c) Readability graph coordinates
    (d) Mugford difficulty index

(a) US school grades

DALE INDEX (ESTIMATED)
FLESCH GRADE EQUIVALENT
FOG INDEX
SMOG H
SMOG X
P–S–K
FORCAST

These measures suggest the US school grade below which the text would be likely to cause extra difficulty. For English schools, it is simplest to add 5 to the score and to treat it as the age in years below which the materials could cause problems. The scores are, of course, only a guide, and the standard error of the formulae varies from ±0.85 grades (FLESCH) to ±1.5 grades (SMOG).

Finally, it must be noted that most of the original formulae specify calculations based on small samples of a text. The STAR program operates on the whole of the input passage, and the necessary adjustments were made to the formulae. The estimated Dale index is derived from the Flesch index by a simple arithmetic rule first reported in the General Motors STAR program. The Dale index (estimated) should therefore *not* be treated as a Dale–Chall score proper: it tends to give slightly lower scores than the Flesch grade level, but these have not been derived from a searching of the Dale 3000-word list.

The General Motors STAR was written in BASIC for a Honeywell 6000 series computer. STAR was rewritten at Nottingham University in FORTRAN, and several additional measures were incorporated. Finally, the Nottingham University version was rewritten at Middlesex Polytechnic. In this version, some errors are removed, the text analysis is more effective, and computing facilities are used more efficiently.

(b) 'Reading ease' Score
FLESCH INDEX

F–J–P INDEX

These measures give a 'reading ease' score (see Flesch, 1948) out of 100. The lower the score the harder the passage.

(c) Fry graph coordinates
The Fry graph (Fry, 1977) is well known in the reading field. The coordinates, representing number of syllables per word and mean number of sentences per 100 words, plot a point on a graph divided into sections, each section representing one school grade.

(d) Mugford difficulty index
This British formula, originally constructed on an intuitive basis, has been revised and improved over the years, and fared well in terms of reliability and age level accuracy in the Effective Use of Reading validation study (Lunzer and Gardner, 1979). The difficulty index can be read as an age level score up to a score of 15.

Preparation of the data

The text to be analysed must conform to certain standards. (In what follows, for 'card', read 'card or line'.)

Definition of a word. A word is a sequence of letters delimited (separated from the following material) by spaces, or the start or end of a card (so it is not necessary to start or finish a card with a space). Words should not be broken between one card and the next. Punctuation marks do not act as delimiters, therefore all punctuation marks should be followed by a space or be the last character on the card.

The Nottingham University version of STAR counted punctuation marks directly following a word as part of the word, and thus overestimated the average number of letters per word. This fault has been corrected in the Middlesex Polytechnic version of STAR.

Definition of a sentence. A sentence is a sequence of words terminated by one of the following punctuation marks: . (full stop), ? (question mark), ! (exclamation mark), ; (semicolon), : (colon). In general, it is better to avoid using full stops in abbreviated words as these may be taken as terminating the sentence. This causes the average number of words per sentence to be underestimated and the number of sentences to be overestimated. The Middlesex Polytechnic version of STAR attempts to reduce this risk by treating all full stops following words which do not contain any vowels (see below) as indicating abbreviations rather than the end of a sentence. It has been found in practice that there is a tendency for the final full stop in a piece of text to be omitted, so the end of text is recognised as a sentence terminator in this version of STAR.

Definition of a syllable. The number of syllables in a word is defined to be the number of vowels or diphthongs in the word after the following suffices have been removed: . . .*e* (with the exception of . . .*le*), . . .*ed*, . . .*es*, . . .*eed*, and . . .*ees*. The letter *y* is treated as a vowel except when it is the first letter in the word.

Structure of the input data file

Several passages may be analysed during one run of the program. Each passage begins with a card that controls the output to be produced. This card consists of two items of data. If YES is punched in columns 1–3, then the input text will be listed. If YES is punched in columns 4–6, then HI-CAL words will be listed. A HI-CAL word is a word containing three or more syllables. If the first card does not contain YES in either columns 1–3 or columns 4–6, then the first card will be taken as text.

A passage is terminated by a card containing # # # in columns 1–3. This card normally follows the last card of the passage. If a further text passage follows, this will normally be headed by the header card described above. The last (or only) text passage need not be followed by a # # # card.

The following example illustrates the make up of a data file for STAR.

YESYES

THIS IS AN EXAMPLE OF TEXT WHICH MAY BE ANALYSED BY THE STAR PROGRAM. THIS WILL BE PRINTED BY STAR AS IT IS PRE-CEDED BY A CARD CONTAINING YES IN COLUMNS 1–3. THE HI-CAL WORDS WILL ALSO BE PRINTED AS COLUMNS 4–6 OF THE CARD CONTAIN YES.

# # #

YES

THIS IS A SECOND PIECE OF TEXT FOR PROCESSING BY STAR. THE ANALYSIS BY STAR WILL NOT LIST THE HI-CAL WORDS BECAUSE COLUMNS 4–6 OF THE HEADER CARD DO NOT CONTAIN YES.

# # #

THIS IS A THIRD PASSAGE OF TEXT. AS THE HEADER CARD IS OMITTED, THE ONLY OUTPUT FROM STAR WILL BE THE LISTING OF THE LINGUISTIC VARIABLES COMPUTED BY STAR AND THE ESTIMATES OF READABILITY DERIVED FROM LINGUISTIC MEAS-URES.

ALTHOUGH THIS SENTENCE IS NOT FOLLOWED BY A FULL STOP, STAR WILL NOT MISCOUNT THE SENTENCES IN THIS PASSAGE

```
C
C-----------------------------------------------------------------------
C                        *** S  T  A  R ***
C=======================================================================
C
C                    Text Readability Estimation
C
C=======================================================================
C    Program to evaluate arithmetic estimates  of   the   readability  of
C    text, based on General Motors BASIC program.
C                             Source:-
C    Colin Harrison, School of Education, University  of Nottingham.
C
C                         Original Version
C                      Programmer:- G P Walker
C                           27-Jan-75
C
C
C          Second Version, including Mugford formula
C                    Programmer:- Sue Davies
C              Second version produced June 1977
C
C-----------------------------------------------------------------------
C
C                    Converted for DECsystem 10 by:
C                         Derek J Bush
C                      Middlesex Polytechnic
C
C                         November 1978
C
C-----------------------------------------------------------------------
C
```

```
STAR - Text Readability Estimation Program                    Page 2
Main Program


        DOUBLE PRECISION FILENM, VERSN
C
        INTEGER ASTRK1, ASTRSK, BLANK, DAYT (2), ENDLIN, HASH, HASH1,
       1        INFILE, JOBNO, OUTFIL, SCRFIL, SLASH, SLASH1, SMOGH,
       2        START, TEXT (80), TYME, WDSYLS, YES
C
C
        LOGICAL ENDSW, HICLSW, LCOMP, LSNIND, SCRMPT, SNTIND, TEXTSW
C
        REAL MUGRDL, MUGWLS
C
C
        COMMON DAYT, FILENM, INFILE, OUTFIL, SCRFIL, TYME
C
C
        DATA ASTRSK, BLANK, HASH,  SLASH, YES/
       1     '***',  ' ',   '£££', '///', 'YES'/
C
        DATA ASTRK1, HASH1, SLASH1 /
       1     '*',    '£',   '/'    /
C
        DATA ENDLIN, ENDSW,   JOBNO, SCRMPT /
       1     80,     .FALSE., 1,     .TRUE. /
C
C *** Version Number follows:
C
        DATA VERSN / '2.10(23)' /
C       ************************
C
C
C
C
C *** System conversion note: changes to Device numbers should be made below.
C       ======================
C       **********
        INFILE = 1
        OUTFIL = 20
        SCRFIL = 21
C       **********
C
C
C       System conversion note:  initialisations which  use  DECsystem  10
C       routines  to  obtain the name of the Input File (FILENM), the date
C       (DAYT) and time (TYME) are contained in  DEC10  subroutine.  These
C       should  be  replaced  by  equivalent routines in Host system. Note
C       that FILENM in this version is DOUBLE PRECISION and  contains  'A'
C       format characters.
C
C       ****************
        CALL DEC10 ( 1 )
C       ****************
C
C
C
C *** Read first card, initialize parameters
C
        READ (1, 235, END = 225) PNTEXT, PNHICL
```

```
    100 NSNTNC = 0
        NWORDS = 0
        NSYLBL = 0
        NCHARS = 0
        NHCW = 0
        N1SW = 0
        LSNIND = .FALSE.
        TEXTSW = .FALSE.
        HICLSW = .FALSE.
        MUGPAR = 0
        IF ( LCOMP (PNTEXT, YES) ) TEXTSW = .TRUE.
        IF ( LCOMP (PNHICL, YES) ) HICLSW = .TRUE.
        IF ( TEXTSW) WRITE (OUTFIL, 240) VERSN, DAYT, TYME, JOBNO, FILENM
        IF ( TEXTSW .OR. HICLSW) GO TO 105
        REREAD 255, (TEXT (I), I = 1,ENDLIN)
        GO TO 110
C
    105 READ (INFILE, 255, END = 160) (TEXT (I), I=1, ENDLIN)
C
    110 IF ( LCOMP (TEXT (1), HASH1) ) GO TO 165
        IF ( LCOMP (TEXT (1), ASTRK1) ) GO TO 160
C
C *** Find last non space character.
C
        DO 115 I = ENDLIN,1,-1
            IF ( LCOMP (TEXT (I), BLANK) ) GO TO 115
            LSTCHR = I
            GO TO 120
    115 CONTINUE
C
C *** Blank line, read another.
C
        GO TO 105
C
    120 IF ( TEXTSW) WRITE (OUTFIL, 260) (TEXT (I), I = 1, LSTCHR)
C
C *** Find first non BLANK character.
C
        START = 1
    125 DO 130 I = START, LSTCHR
            IF ( LCOMP (TEXT (I), BLANK) ) GO TO 130
            IF ( LCOMP (TEXT (I), ASTRK1) .OR. LCOMP (TEXT (I), SLASH1) )
        1       GO TO 130
            START = I
            GO TO 135
    130 CONTINUE
C
C
C *** Find next BLANK character
C
    135 DO 145 I = START, LSTCHR
            IF ( LCOMP (TEXT (I), BLANK) ) GO TO 140
            IF ( .NOT. LCOMP (TEXT (I), ASTRSK) .AND.
        1       .NOT. LCOMP (TEXT (I), SLASH) ) GO TO 145
```

```
   140       LAST = I - 1
             GO TO 150
   145 CONTINUE
         LAST = LSTCHR
C
C *** Word contained in TEXT (START) to TEXT (LAST).
C *** Examine each 'word' with ICOUNT to determine various counts.
C
   150 LENGTH = LAST - START + 1
         CALL ICOUNT (TEXT (START), LENGTH, WDSYLS, SNTIND, LETTRS)
C
C *** Increment sentence count if not ellipis.
C
         IF (SNTIND .AND. .NOT. LSNIND) NSNTNC = NSNTNC + 1
         LSNIND = SNTIND
C
C *** Skip if 'word' contained only non-alphabetics.
C
         IF (LETTRS .EQ. 0) GO TO 155
C
C *** Increment appropriate counts for this 'word'.
C
         NWORDS = NWORDS + 1
         NCHARS = NCHARS + LETTRS
         NSYLBL = NSYLBL + WDSYLS
         IF (WDSYLS .GE. 3) NHCW = NHCW + 1
         IF (WDSYLS .EQ. 1) N1SW = N1SW + 1
         CALL MFD (WDSYLS, LETTRS, MUGPAR)
         IF ( .NOT. HICLSW) GO TO 155
         IF (WDSYLS .LT. 3) GO TO 155
C
C *** Stack Hi-cal words on Scratch File.
C
         WRITE (SCRFIL, 265) LENGTH, WDSYLS, (TEXT (I), I = START,LAST)
         SCRMPT = .FALSE.
   155 IF (LAST .EQ. LSTCHR) GO TO 105
         START = LAST + 1
C
C *** Return for next 'word'.
C
         GO TO 125
C
C *** Entry if last passage identified.
C
   160 ENDSW = .TRUE.
C
C *** End of a passage found, compute and report indices.
C
C
C *** Trap if last line of passage did not finish with a period.
C
   165 IF ( .NOT. LSNIND ) NSNTNC = NSNTNC + 1
C
C *** Exit if no words found in passage.
```

```
C
      IF ( NWORDS .EQ. 0 ) GO TO 215
C
C
C *** Write Final Results to File.
C
      WRITE (OUTFIL, 250) VERSN, DAYT, TYME, JOBNO, FILENM
C
C *** Calculate Words/Sentences, Syllables/Word
C
      WDPSNT = FLOAT (NWORDS)/FLOAT (NSNTNC)
      SYPWRD = FLOAT (NSYLBL)/FLOAT (NWORDS)
C
C *** Calculate Flesch & Dale Index
C
      FLESCH = 206.835 - 1.015*WDPSNT - 84.6*SYPWRD
      DALE = 11.534 - 0.053*FLESCH
C
C *** Calculate Chars/Word, Chars/Sentence
C
      CHPWRD = FLOAT (NCHARS)/FLOAT (NWORDS)
      CHPSNT = FLOAT (NCHARS)/FLOAT (NSNTNC)
C
C *** Calculate Fog Index, Smog-h, PSK, FJP, FRY  co-ords, Forcast
C
      FOGIND=0.4*(WDPSNT + 100.0*FLOAT (NHCW)/FLOAT (NWORDS))
      SMOGX = SQRT (30.0*FLOAT (NHCW)/FLOAT (NSNTNC)) + 3.0
      SMOGH = SMOGX + 0.5
      PSKIND = 4.55 * SYPWRD + 0.0778 * WDPSNT - 2.2029
      FJPIND = 159.9*FLOAT (N1SW)/FLOAT (NWORDS) - 1.015*WDPSNT - 31.517
      FRYX = 100.0*FLOAT (NSNTNC)/FLOAT (NWORDS)
      FRYY = 100.0*SYPWRD
      FORCST = 20.43 - 16.5*FLOAT (N1SW)/FLOAT (NWORDS)
C
C ***  Calculate Mugford Readability formula
C
      MUGRDL = 2.0673*FLOAT (MUGPAR)/FLOAT (NWORDS) + 0.1172*WDPSNT +
     1         6.4636
      MUGWLS = 0.5*FLOAT (MUGPAR)
      WRITE (OUTFIL, 275) CHPWRD, CHPSNT
      WRITE (OUTFIL, 280) NSNTNC, NWORDS, NSYLBL
      WRITE (OUTFIL, 285) N1SW, NHCW
      WRITE (OUTFIL, 290) WDPSNT, SYPWRD, FLESCH, DALE
      IF ( FLESCH .LT. 60.0 ) GO TO 175
      IF ( FLESCH .LT. 70.0 ) GO TO 170
      FLGRD = (150.0 - FLESCH )/10.0
      GO TO 185
  170 FLGRD = (110.0 - FLESCH)/5.0
      GO TO 185
  175 IF ( FLESCH .LT. 50.0 ) GO TO 180
      FLGRD = (93.0 - FLESCH)/3.333
      GO TO 185
  180 FLGRD = (140.0 - FLESCH)/6.66
  185 WRITE (OUTFIL, 295) FLGRD
```

STAR - Text Readability Estimation Program   Page 6
Main Program

```
      WRITE (OUTFIL, 300) FOGIND, SMOGH, SMOGX, PSKIND
      WRITE (OUTFIL, 305) FJPIND, FRYX, FRYY
      WRITE (OUTFIL, 310) FORCST
      WRITE (OUTFIL, 315) MUGRDL, MUGWLS
C
C *** If Hi-cal words found, transfer from Scratch File to Output File.
C
      IF ( SCRMPT ) GO TO 200
      SCRMPT = .TRUE.
      END FILE SCRFIL
      REWIND SCRFIL
C     ****************
      CALL DEC10 ( 2 )
C     ****************
      WRITE (OUTFIL,245) VERSN, DAYT, TYME, JOBNO, FILENM
C
C *** Transfer loop.
C
  190 READ (SCRFIL,265,END=195) LENGTH, WDSYLS, (TEXT (I), I = 1,LENGTH)
      WRITE (OUTFIL, 270) WDSYLS, (TEXT (I), I = 1,LENGTH)
      GO TO 190
C
C *** All Hi-cal words transferred, rewind Scratch File for next passage
C
  195 REWIND SCRFIL
C     ****************
      CALL DEC10 ( 3 )
C     ****************
      SCRMPT = .TRUE.
C
C *** Update Job count by one
C
  200 JOBNO = JOBNO + 1
C
C *** Skip if all passages processed.
C
      IF (ENDSW) GO TO 210
C
C *** else, look at first card of next passage.
C
  205 READ (INFILE, 235, END = 210) PNTEXT, PNHICL
      IF ( LCOMP (PNTEXT, HASH) ) GO TO 205
      IF ( LCOMP (PNTEXT, ASTRSK) ) GO TO 210
      GO TO 100
C     ****************
  210 CALL DEC10 ( 4 )
C     ****************
      STOP    .
C
C *** Error - no data found in current passage
C
  215 WRITE (OUTFIL, 220) JOBNO
  220 FORMAT ('0No data found in passage of Job ',I3,
     1         '0Skipping to next passage')
```

```
         GO TO 200
C
C *** Error - no data in input file!
C
   225 TYPE 230
   230 FORMAT ('0No data found in input file, run aborts')
C        ****************
         CALL DEC10 ( 5 )
C        ****************
         STOP
C
C
C *** FORMAT statements follow
C
   235 FORMAT (2A3)
   240 FORMAT ('1STAR V', A10, 16X, 'S  T  A  R'/1X, 2A5, 1X, A5, 14X,
      1        15('*')// 6X, 'Input Text for Job number ', I3,
      2        ' from file ', A10/)
   245 FORMAT ('1STAR V', A10, 16X, 'S  T  A  R'/1X, 2A5, 1X, A5, 14X,
      1        15('*')//1X,'Listing of HI-CAL Words for Job number ',I3,
      2        ' from file ', A10/)
   250 FORMAT ('1STAR V', A10, 16X, 'S  T  A  R'/1X, 2A5, 1X, A5, 14X,
      1        15('*')//6X,'Final Results for Job number ', I3,
      2        ' from file ', A10/)
   255 FORMAT (80A1)
   260 FORMAT (1X, 80A1)
   265 FORMAT (I2,I3,80A1)
   270 FORMAT (6X,I3,5X,80A1)
   275 FORMAT (9X, 'Characters per Word =', F8.2/
      1        5X, 'Characters per Sentence =', F8.2)
   280 FORMAT (9X,'Number of Sentences =',I5/
      1        13X, 'Number of Words =',I5/
      2        9X,'Number of Syllables =',I5)
   285 FORMAT (5X,'Number of monosyllabics =',I5/
      1        4X,'Number of high-cal words =',I5)
   290 FORMAT (1H , 4X, 'Average Sentence Length =', F8.2/
      1        2X, 'Average Syllables per Word =', F8.2///
      2        16X, 'Flesch Index =',F8.2/
      3        7X, 'Dale Index (estimate) =', F8.2)
   295 FORMAT (5X, 'Flesch Grade Equivalent =', F8.2)
   300 FORMAT (19X, 'FOG Index =', F8.2/
      1        16X,'SMOG-H Index =',I5/
      2        16X,'SMOG-X Index =',F8.2/
      3        17X, 'P-S-K Index =', F8.2)
   305 FORMAT (17X, 'F-J-P Index =', F8.2/
      1        16X, 'Fry Co-ord-X =', F8.2/
      2        16X, 'Fry Co-ord-Y =', F8.2)
   310 FORMAT (15X, 'Forcast Grade =', F8.2)
   315 FORMAT (7X, 'Mugford Reading Level =', F8.2/
      1        11X, 'Mugford WL. Score =', F7.1)
         END
```

```
         LOGICAL FUNCTION LCOMP (VAL1, VAL2)
C
C        Function  LCOMP  takes the value .TRUE. if argument VAL1 is found
C        be identical with argument VAL2.
C
         INTEGER VAL1, VAL2
C
C
C
         LCOMP=(VAL1 .EQ. VAL2)
         RETURN
         END
```

```
      SUBROUTINE ICOUNT (TEXT, LENGTH, NSYLLS, SNTIND, LETTRS)
C
C     This SUBROUTINE carries out the detailed examination of each
C     string found by the MAIN program. A string is defined as a group
C     of characters delimited by SPACEs or End of Line characters.
C
C     Arguments:
C          TEXT    points to the first character in the string
C          LENGTH  contains the number of characters contained in the
C                  string as supplied by calling routine.
C          NSYLLS  returns the number of Vowels or Diphthongs discovered
C                  in the string after the following suffices have been
C                  removed: ..E (with the exception of ..LE), ..ED, ..ES
C                  ..EED, and ..EES.
C          SNTIND  is set to .TRUE. if end of sentence discovered in the
C                  text; a sentence end is when a period (or period
C                  equivalent (? ! ; :) is discovered in the current
C                  string. SNTIND is set .FALSE. if no period is found.
C          LETTRS  returns the number of Letters found in the string.
C
C
C
      INTEGER COMMA, PERIOD (5), QUOTE (2), START, TEXT (LENGTH),
     1        VOWEL (6)
C
      LOGICAL LCOMP, PRVWL, SNTIND, SFXIND
C
C
      DATA COMMA, LTRD, LTRE, LTRL, LTRS /
     1      ',',   'D',  'E',  'L',  'S' /
C
      DATA PERIOD / '.', '?', '!', ':', ';' /
C
      DATA QUOTE / '''', '"' /
C
      DATA VOWEL / 'E', 'A', 'I', 'O', 'U', 'Y' /
C
C
C
C *** Initialisation.
C
      SNTIND = .FALSE.
      LAST = LENGTH
C
C *** Test for Trailing COMMA, APOSTROPHE or QUOTE
C
  100 IF ( .NOT. LCOMP (TEXT (LAST), COMMA) .AND.
     1       .NOT. LCOMP (TEXT (LAST), QUOTE (1) ) .AND.
     2       .NOT. LCOMP (TEXT (LAST), QUOTE (2) ) ) GO TO 105
      LAST = LAST - 1
      GO TO 100
C
C *** Test for end of Sentence
C
```

```
  105 DO 110 I = 1, 5
            IF ( .NOT. LCOMP (TEXT (LAST), PERIOD (I) ) ) GO TO   110
               SNTIND = .TRUE.
               LAST = LAST - 1
               GO TO 100
  110 CONTINUE
C
C *** Test for leading APOSTROPHE or QUOTE
C
      LQUOTE = 0
      IF ( LCOMP (TEXT (1), QUOTE (1) ) .OR.
     1     LCOMP (TEXT (1), QUOTE (2) ) ) LQUOTE = LQUOTE + 1
C
C *** Test if Word contains more than 3 Letters
C *** If not assume 1 Syllable
C
      START = LQUOTE + 1
      LETTRS = LAST - LQUOTE
      IF (LETTRS .GT. 3) GO TO 120
      NSYLLS = 0
      IF ( LETTRS .EQ. 0 ) RETURN
C
C *** If word contains no vowel, then period is probably  not  sentence
C     delimiter.
C
      NSYLLS = 1
      IF ( .NOT. SNTIND ) RETURN
      DO 115 I = START, LAST
            DO 115 J = 1,6
                IF ( LCOMP ( TEXT (I), VOWEL (J) ) ) RETURN
  115 CONTINUE
      SNTIND = .FALSE.
      RETURN
C
C
  120 NSYLLS = 0
C
C ***   Test for Suffixes
C
      SFXIND = .FALSE.
      IF ( .NOT. LCOMP (TEXT (LAST - 1),LTRE) ) GO TO 125
      IF ( LCOMP (TEXT (LAST), LTRD) ) GO TO 130
      IF ( LCOMP (TEXT (LAST), LTRS) ) GO TO 130
  125 IF ( LCOMP (TEXT (LAST - 1), LTRL) ) GO TO 140
      GO TO 135
  130 LAST = LAST - 2
C
C ***   Test for Trailing 'E'
C
  135 IF ( .NOT. LCOMP (TEXT (LAST), LTRE) )  GO TO 140
      LAST = LAST - 1
      SFXIND = .TRUE.
  140 PRVWL = .FALSE.
C
```

STAR - Text Readability Estimation Program   Page 11
ICOUNT

```
C *** Count number of Vowels/Diphthongs.
C
      DO 150 I = START, LAST
         DO 145 J = 1, 6

               IF ( PRVWL ) GO TO 150
               PRVWL = .TRUE.
               NSYLLS = NSYLLS + 1
               GO TO 150
  145    CONTINUE
         PRVWL = .FALSE.
  150 CONTINUE
C
C *** Reduce probability of treating abbreviation-periods as sentence
C *** delimiter.
C
      IF ( NSYLLS .GT. 0 ) RETURN
C
C *** Syllables zero but suffices have been stripped, so NSYLLS = 1
C
      IF ( SFXIND ) GO TO 155
C
C *** Syllables zero, no suffices stripped, so probable abbreviation
C     and any period should be treated as false.
C
      SNTIND = .FALSE.
C
  155 NSYLLS = 1
      RETURN
C
      END
```

STAR - Text Readability Estimation Program   Page 12
MFD

```
      SUBROUTINE MFD (NSYLLS, NCHAR, MUGPAR)
C
C     This subroutine increments the Mugford parameter value (MUGPAR)
C     depending on the nature of the word encountered.
C
C     If the number of Mugford syllables > 2    increment is 8
C     If the number of Mugford syllables < 3,
C     then, if the number of letters < 5        increment is 0
C            if the number of letters = 5       increment is 2
C            if the number of letters = 6       increment is 3
C            if the number of letters > 6       increment is 5
C
      IF (NSYLLS .GT. 2) GO TO 105
      K = NCHAR - 3
      IF ( K .GT. 3 ) GO TO 100
      IF ( K .LT. 2 ) RETURN
      GO TO 110
C
  100 K = 5
      GO TO 110
C
  105 K = 8
  110 MUGPAR = MUGPAR + K
      RETURN
C
      END
```

```
      SUBROUTINE DEC10 ( MODE )
C
C     Subroutine  DEC10  contains  all  the  specialised  DECsystem   10
C     routines  which are unique to DECsystem 10 (or 20) FORTRAN.  These
C     routines  are  maintained  in  this  subroutine  in  order  that
C     conversion  of  this  program  to  run  on  another manufacturer's
C     computer system will be as painless as possible. At the same time,
C     the advantages of using the DECsystem 10 routines are retained for
C     DECsystem 10 (or 20) users.
C
C     Arguments:
C     MODE      indicates the mode of operation required from DEC10:
C               if MODE = 1: File opening routines are carried out,
C               if MODE = 2: Switching of Scratch File from write to  read
C                            is undertaken, and
C               if MODE = 3: Switching of Scratch File from read to  write
C                            is undertaken, and
C               if MODE = 4: File closing routines are carried out, and
C               if MODE = 5: Abort routine without printing.
C
C     Values returned through COMMON:
C     FILENM    is  a double precision variable which contains the name of
C               the Input file on exit. This is provided  to  the  calling
C               program  in  order that the name of the file may appear on
C               the Output listing.
C     DAYT      is  an  INTEGER  array  (2 locations)  which  contains the
C               current date in '2A5' format on exit.
C     TYME      is  an  INTEGER  variable  which contains the current time
C               in 'A5' format on exit.
C
C
      DOUBLE PRECISION DBLANK, FILENM
C
C
      LOGICAL OUTAPP
C
C
      INTEGER DAYT (2), SCRFIL, OUTFIL, TYME
C
C
      COMMON DAYT, FILENM, INFILE, OUTFIL, SCRFIL, TYME
C
C
      DATA DBLANK / ' ' /
C
C
C
C *** Go to appropriate routine.
C
      GO TO ( 100, 140, 145, 150, 150), MODE
C
C *** Opening routines
C
C
```

```
C *** Get Date and Time.
C
   100 FILENM = 'STAR.TXT'
       CALL DATE (DAYT)
       CALL TIME (TYME)
C
C
C *** Open all files, get name of input file if not STAR.TXT
C
   105 OPEN (UNIT=INFILE,DEVICE='DSK',ACCESS='SEQIN',FILE=FILENM,ERR=110)
       GO TO 125
C *** Interrogate for input file name if file STAR.TXT not found
   110 TYPE 115, FILENM
   115 FORMAT ('0File ', A10, ' not found.'/'0Type in name of input file'
      1/'0Type RETURN key to abort'//)
       ACCEPT 120, FILENM
   120 FORMAT (A10)
       IF (FILENM .EQ. DBLANK) STOP
       GO TO 105
C
C      Open output files in APPEND mode, so that previously spooled files
C      which have not yet been printed are not overwritten.
C
   125 OUTAPP = .FALSE.
       OPEN (UNIT=OUTFIL,DEVICE='DSK',FILE='STARZ1.DAT',ACCESS='SEQIN',
      1      ERR=130)
       OUTAPP = .TRUE.
       CLOSE (UNIT=OUTFIL)
   130 OPEN (UNIT=OUTFIL,DEVICE='DSK',FILE='STARZ1.DAT',ACCESS='APPEND')
       OPEN (UNIT=SCRFIL,DEVICE='DSK',FILE='STARZ2.DAT',ACCESS='SEQOUT')
       TYPE 135, FILENM
   135 FORMAT ('0Commencing analysis of ',A10)
       RETURN
C
C
C *** Switch over of Scratch File from write to read.
C
   140 CLOSE (UNIT=SCRFIL)
       OPEN (UNIT=SCRFIL,DEVICE='DSK',FILE='STARZ2.DAT',ACCESS='SEQIN')
       RETURN
C
C *** Switch over from read to write.
C
   145 CLOSE (UNIT=SCRFIL,DISPOSE='DELETE')
       OPEN (UNIT=SCRFIL,DEVICE='DSK',FILE='STARZ2.DAT',ACCESS='SEQOUT')
       RETURN
C
C
C *** Closing routines.
C
   150 CLOSE (UNIT = INFILE)
       CLOSE (UNIT=SCRFIL, DISPOSE = 'DELETE')
       IF ( OUTAPP ) GO TO 155
       IF ( MODE .EQ. 5 ) GO TO 160
```

```
      CLOSE (UNIT=OUTFIL, DISPOSE = 'LIST')
      RETURN
  155 CLOSE (UNIT=OUTFIL, DISPOSE='SAVE')
      RETURN
C
C *** Abort run, do not print output file.
C
  160 CLOSE (UNIT=OUTFIL, DISPOSE='DELETE')
      RETURN
C
      END
```

Bibliography

Anderson R. C. (1972) How to construct achievement tests to assess comprehension. *Review of Educational Research* 42, 2, 145–70.

Atkinson E. T. and Gains C. W. (1973) *Reading: A-Z.* Birmingham: National Association for Remedial Education.

Ausubel D. P. (1960) The use of advance organisers in the learning and retention of meaningful verbal material. *Journal of Educational Psychology* 51, 267–72.

Bloomer R. H. (1966) Non-overt reinforced cloze procedure. *USOE Cooperative Research Project* 2245. University of Connecticut.

Bormuth J. R. (1965a) Comparisons among cloze test scoring methods. In J. A. Figurel (Ed.) *Reading and Inquiry.* Newark, Delaware: International Reading Association.

Bormuth J. R. (1965b) Optimum sample size and cloze test length in readability measurement. *Journal of Educational Measurement* 2, 1, 111–16.

Bormuth J. R. (1966) Readability: a new approach. *Reading Research Quarterly* I/3, 79–132.

Bormuth J. R. (1968) Cloze test readability: criterion reference scores. *Journal of Educational Measurement* 5, 189–96.

Bormuth J. R. (1969a) *Development of Readability Analyses.* Final report, project 7-0052, Bureau of Research, USOE.

Bormuth J. R. (1969b) Empirical determination of the instructional reading level. In J. A. Figurel (Ed.) *Reading and Realism.* Newark, Delaware: International Reading Association.

Botel M. and Granowsky A. (1972) A formula for measuring syntactic complexity: a directional effort. *Elementary English* 59 (April), 513–16.

Call R. J. and Wiggin N. A. (1974) Reading and Mathematics. In Hafner L. E. (Ed.) *Improving Reading in Middle and Secondary Schools.* New York: Macmillan, 333–346.

Carroll J. B. (1971) *Learning from Verbal Discourse in Educational Media: A Review of the Literature.* Princeton, N.J.: Educational Testing Service (USOE) 125–6, 160–1.

Carroll J. B. (1972) Defining language comprehension: some

speculations. In Freedle R. O. and Carroll J. B. (Eds.) *Language Comprehension and the Acquisition of Knowledge*. New York: Wiley.

Carver R. P. (1975–76) Measuring prose difficulty using the Rauding scale. *Reading Research Quarterly* XI, 4, 660–685.

Chall, Jeanne S. (1958) *Readability – An Appraisal of Research and Application*. Columbus, Ohio: Bureau of Educational Research, Ohio State University.

Chomsky N. (1957) *Syntactic Structures*. The Hague: Mouton.

Chomsky N. (1965) *Aspects of the Theory of Syntax*. Cambridge, Mass: M.I.T. Press.

Cohen Judith H. (1975) The effect of content area material on cloze test performance. *Journal of Reading* 19, 3, 247–50. December 1975.

Coleman E. B. (1968) Experimental studies of readability. *Elementary English* 45, 166–78.

Dale E. and Chall J. S. (1948) A formula for predicting readability. *Educational Research Bulletin* 27, 11–20, 37–54.

Dawkins J. (1975) *Syntax and Readability*. Newark, Delaware: International Reading Association.

Department of Education and Science (1975) *A Language for Life* (The Bullock report). London: HMSO.

Elley W. B. (1969) The assessment of readability by noun frequency counts. *Reading Research Quarterly* IV, 411–27.

Flesch R. F. (1948) A new readability yardstick. *Journal of Applied Psychology* 32, 221–33.

Flesch R. F. (1950) Measuring the level of abstraction. *Journal of Applied Psychology* 34, 384–90.

Fry E. (1977) Fry's readability graph: clarification, validity and extension to level 17. *Journal of Reading* 20, December, 242–52.

Golub L. S. and Kidder C. (1974) Syntactic density and the computer. *Elementary English* 51, 8, 1128–31.

Graham W. (1978) Readability and science textbooks. *School Science Review* 59/208, March, 545–50.

Gunning R. (1952) *The Technique of Clear Writing*. New York: McGraw-Hill.

Harrison C. (1977a) Assessing the readability of school texts. In Gilliland J. (Ed.) *Reading: Research and Classroom Practice* London: Ward Lock Educational.

Harrison C. (1977b) Cloze test comprehension scores on two versions of a document on the driving test. Unpublished research report for the Transport and Road Research Laboratory, Crowthorne, Berkshire. Dated February 1977.

Harrison C. (1979) Assessing the readability of school texts. In Lunzer E. A. and Gardner W. K. (Eds.) *The Effective Use of Reading*. London: Heinemann.

Hill L. E. (1978) A readability study of school library provision related to children's interests and reading abilities. Unpublished dissertation. University of London Institute of Education.

Huey E. B. (1968) *The Psychology and Pedagogy of Reading* (reprinted). Cambridge, Mass: M.I.T. Press.

Jongsma E. (1971) *The Cloze Procedure as a Teaching Technique.* Newark, Delaware: International Reading Association.

Kane R., Hater M. A. and Byrne M. A. (1974) *Helping Children Read Mathematics.* New York: American Book Co.

Kennedy D. K. and Weener P. (1973) Visual and auditory training with the Cloze procedure to improve reading and listening comprehension. *Reading Research Quarterly* VIII/4, 524–41.

Kingston A. J. (ed.) (1977) *Toward a Psychology of Reading and Language: Selected Writings of Wendell W. Weaver.* Athens: University of Georgia Press.

Kintsch W. (1974) *The Representation of Meaning in Memory.* Hillsdale, N. J.: Erlbaum.

Kintsch W., Kozminsky E., Streby W. J., McKoon G. and Keenan J. M. (1975) Comprehension and recall of text as a function of content variables. *Journal of Verbal Learning and Verbal Behaviour* 14, 196–214.

Klare, G. R. (1963) *The Measurement of Readability.* Ames: Iowa State University Press.

Klare G. R. (1975a) Judging readability. *Instructional Science* 5, 55–61.

Klare G. R. (1975b) *A Manual for Readable Writing.* Glen Burnie, Maryland: REM Company.

Klare G. R. (1976) A second look at the validity of readability formulas. *Journal of Reading Behaviour* 8, 2, 129–52.

Klare G. R., Sinaiko H. W. and Stolurow L. M. (1972) The cloze procedure: a convenient readability test for training materials and translations. *International Review of Applied Psychology* 21, 2, 77–106.

Kolers P. A. (1973) The three stages of reading. In Smith F. (Ed.) (1973) *Psycholinguistics and Reading.* New York: Holt, Rinehart and Winston, p. 47.

Kučera H. and Francis W. N. (1967) *Computational Analysis of Present Day American English.* Providence R. I. Brown University Press.

Longley C. (Ed.) (1975) *BBC Adult Literacy Handbook.* London: BBC Publications.

Longley C. (Ed.) (1977) *Reading After Ten.* London: BBC Publications.

Lunzer E. A. and Gardner W. K. (Eds.) (1979) *The Effective Use of Reading.* Schools Council Project Report. London: Heinemann.

MacGinitie W. H. (1961) Contextual constraint in English prose paragraphs. *Journal of Psychology* 51, 121–30.

Mandler Jean M. and Johnson Nancy S. (1977) Remembrance of things parsed: story structure and recall. *Cognitive Psychology* 9, 1, 111–51.

MacDonald-Ross M. and Smith E. B. (1973) *Bibliography for Textural Communication.* Monograph number 3. Milton Keynes: Institute of Educational Technology, The Open University.

Maginnis G. H. (1969) The readability graph and informal reading inventories. *The Reading Teacher* 22/6, 516–18 and 559.

McCall W. A. and Crabbs L. M. (1925) *Standard Test Lessons in Reading.* New York: Teachers' College, Columbia University.

McCullagh S. K. (1969) *Johnny and Jennifer Yellow-Hat.* London: Hart-Davis Educational.

McLaughlin G. (1969) SMOG grading – a new readability formula. *Journal of Reading* 22, 639–46.

McLeod J. (1970) *Manual: Gap Reading Comprehension Test.* London: Heinemann.

McLeod J. and Anderson J. (1973) *Manual: Gapadol Reading Comprehension Test.* London: Heinemann.

Miller L. R. (1975) Predictive powers of multiple-choice and cloze-derived readability formulas. *Reading Improvement* 12, 1, 52–58. Spring 1975.

Moon C. and Raban B. (1975) *A Question of Reading.* London: Ward Lock Educational (second edition, London: Macmillan 1980).

Mugford L. (1970) A new way of predicting readability. *Reading* 4, 2, 31–5.

Neville M. H. and Pugh A. K. (1976–77) Context in reading and listening: variations in approach to cloze tasks. *Reading Research Quarterly* XII/1, 13–31.

NFER (1977) *Reading Level Tests.* Windsor: NFER Publishing Company.

Powers R. D., Sumner W. A. and Kearl B. E. (1958) A recalculation of four readability formulas. *Journal of Educational Psychology* 49, 99–105.

Rankin E. F. and Culhane J. W. (1969) Comparable cloze and multiple-choice comprehension test scores. *Journal of Reading* 13, 193–8.

Rosenshine B. (1969) New correlates of readability and listenability. In J. A. Figurel (Ed.) *Reading and Realism,* 1968 Proceedings, Vol. 13. Part 1. Newark, Delaware: International Reading Association 1969.

Rothkopf E. Z. (1970) The concept of mathemagenic activities. *Review of Educational Research* 40, 325–36.

Shnayer S. W. (1969) Relationships between reading interest and reading comprehension. In J. A. Figurel (Ed.) *Reading and Realism,* 1968 Proceedings, Vol. 13, Part 1. Newark, Delaware: International Reading Association, pp. 698–702.

Smith F. (Ed.) (1973) *Psycholinguistics and Reading.* New York: Holt, Rinehart & Winston.

Smith F. (1978a) *Reading.* Cambridge: Cambridge University Press.

Smith F. (1978b) *Understanding Reading.* Second edition: New York:

Holt, Rinehart & Winston.

Spache G. D. (1953) A new readability formula for primary grade reading materials. *Elementary School Journal* 53, 410–13.

Stenhouse L. (Ed.) (1970, 1973) *Humanities Curriculum Project.* London: Heinemann.

Sticht T. G. (1972) Learning by listening. In Freedle R. O. and Carroll J. B. (Eds.) *Language Comprehension and the Acquisition of Knowledge.* Washington D.C.: Winston.

Sticht T. G. (1973) Research toward the design, development and evaluation of a job-functional literacy program for the us Army. *Literacy Discussion* IV, 3, September 1973, 339–69.

Stokes A. (1978) The reliability of readability formulae. *Journal of Research in Reading* 1, 1, 21–34.

Taylor W. L. (1953) Cloze procedure: a new tool for measuring readability. *Journalism Quarterly* 30, Fall, 415–33.

Thorndike E. L. and Lorge I. (1944) *Teachers' Word Book of 30,000 Words.* New York: Bureau of Publications, Teachers' College, Columbia University.

Tinker M. A. (1963) *Legibility of Print.* Ames: Iowa State University Press.

Trabasso T. (1972) Mental operations in language comprehension. In Freedle R. O. and Carrol J. B. (Eds.) *Language Comprehension and the Acquisition of Knowledge.* New York: Winston/Wiley.

Tuinman J. J. (1973–74) Determining the passage dependency of comprehension questions in 5 major tests. *Reading Research Quarterly* IX/3, 206–223.

Turner B. (1971) An evaluation of written material provided for the Schools Council Humanities Curriculum Project. Unpublished dissertation, Teeside College of Education.

Walker C. (1974) *Reading Development and Extension.* London: Ward Lock Educational.

Watts L. and Nisbet J. (1974) *Legibility in Children's Books – A Review of Research.* Windsor: NFER.

Weaver W. W. (1963) A factor analysis of cloze procedure and other measures of reading and language ability. *Journal of Communications* 13, 252–61. Reprinted in Kingston A. J. (Ed.) 1977, 103–12.

Weaver W. W. (1977a) The predictability of omissions in reading and listening. Reprinted in Kingston A. J. (Ed.) *Toward a Psychology of Reading and Language.* Athens: University of Georgia Press, p. 5.

Weaver W. W. (1977b) Theoretical aspects of the cloze procedure. In Kingston A. J. (Ed.) *Toward a Psychology of Reading and Language.* Athens: University of Georgia Press, p. 16.

Acknowledgements

The author and the publisher wish to thank the following for permission to reproduce material in their copyright.

E. A. Lunzer and W. K. Gardner (Eds.), *The Effective Use of Reading*, Schools Council project report, Heinemann, 1979, for Tables 3.1 and 5.1

Leonard Mugford for Figures 3.1, 3.2 and 3.3

Edward Fry for Figure 3.4

R. F. Flesch, *How to Test Readability*, Harper and Row, for the Flesch formula and Figure 3.5

J. R. Bormuth, *Development of Readability Analyses*, final report, project 7-0052, Bureau of Research, USOE, 1969, for Figure 4.1

J. McLeod, *Manual: Gapadol Reading Comprehension Test*, Heinemann, 1970, for Figure 4.2

G. Klare for the extract on page 142

E. Dale for the word lists and the Dale–Chall formula

D. J. Bush and the Middlesex Polytechnic for the STAR computer program

Index

Paste